Tackling Learning Difficulties

A Whole School Approach

Thomas

TACKLING LEARNING DIFFICULTIES

A Whole School Approach

Edited by Olive Robinson and Gary Thomas

HODDER AND STOUGHTON
LONDON SYDNEY AUCKLAND TORONTO

British Library Cataloguing in Publication Data

Tackling learning difficulties: a whole
school approach.
  1. Schools. Learning disordered students.
  Teaching
  I. Robinson, Olive II. Thomas, Gary
  371.9'043

ISBN 0 340 42674 8

First published 1988

Phototypeset by Gecko Limited, Bicester, Oxon.
Printed in Great Britain for Hodder and Stoughton Educational, a division of
Hodder and Stoughton Limited, Mill Road, Dunton Green, Sevenoaks, Kent
by Richard Clay Ltd, Bungay, Suffolk

Contents

About the Editors

OLIVE ROBINSON has taught both in primary and secondary schools. In the latter sector, she has been involved over a number of years in organising and running special needs departments or units in a variety of schools. She has also worked as a part-time tutor in the education of children with special needs at Oxford University Department of Education and at Oxford Polytechnic. Recently retired from full-time teaching, she is currently engaged in work for Adult Basic Education. Her publications include information books for children and contributions on reading difficulties.

GARY THOMAS has worked as a teacher, an educational psychologist, and a lecturer in special education. He is currently Staff Tutor to two Schools Psychological Services and is an Honorary Research Fellow in the Department of Psychology at University College, London. He has published widely in journals and is co-author of several books on the management of special educational needs.

About the Contributors

JOHN DWYFOR DAVIES has experience working in secondary and special schools, and is currently a Senior Lecturer at Oxford Polytechnic where his main contribution is in supporting a range of courses for teachers on special educational needs. He has published articles on many topics concerning the education of children with special educational needs, both in the UK and abroad, and is presently engaged in editing a book by NFER-Nelson on supporting children with special needs in ordinary schools.

PAT DAVIES has worked for several years in both primary and special schools for children with behaviour and emotional problems. She is currently a Special Needs Advisory and Support Teacher in East Oxfordshire. She has published widely in education journals and books on themes relating to children with learning and behavioural difficulties, and is currently co-editing the book on support teaching with her husband John Davies.

JOHN HOWSON started his teaching career in a comprehensive school in Haringey and studied for his Master's degree after having had experience of working in secondary schools and in a teachers' centre. He is currently Deputy Head of the School of Education at Oxford Polytechnic. His present research interests include the monitoring of headteacher turnover. In 1987 he published a guide to secondary schools in the London area.

RUTH MERTTENS is a Lecturer in Primary Mathematics at the Polytechnic of North London and co-director of the IMPACT Project, a national project involving parents in their children's learning of mathematics. She is both a primary school governor and an active member of her local parent-teacher association. She is a regular contributor to *Junior Education* and is the author of *Teaching Primary Maths* (Edward Arnold).

CAROLINE ROAF is currently Coordinator for Special Needs at Peer's School, Oxford. During a secondment to the Oxford Advisory Centre for Multicultural Education, she made a particular study of whole school policies with reference to the interaction between special needs and multicultural education. She is the co-writer of the Oxon discussion paper on Prejudice and Equality, and her main interests are now concerned with the development of the idea that children's educational needs cannot be effectively met unless educators take into account, and use the concept of, educational rights.

KATY SIMMONS has taught English in schools in both the UK and the USA. After several years of research into reading processes she is now a Senior Lecturer in the School of Education at Oxford Polytechnic. Her main interest is the education of children with special needs: her published work includes research on language, reading development and reading difficulties.

JEFF VASS is a Research Fellow in Education at the Polytechnic of North London and co-director with Ruth Merttens of the IMPACT Project. Following a period teaching in a London comprehensive school, Jeff Vass worked for two years in a primary unit for children with special behaviour and communication difficulties. He has published several papers, the most recent being a contribution to the International Conference on Child Development in Norway.

Introduction

This book is about change and the need for change. There has been much debate in recent years about the future of education, and many changes are now being introduced by government. This book focuses on the changes which have for the last few years been imposing the most immediate and pressing demands on teachers: it looks at the demands placed upon teachers when they are required to educate children of all abilities. In attempting to find ways of meeting those demands, the book examines the development of an approach to special educational needs which is considered not just by the individual teacher but by the whole school community. The assumption held is that the development of such a whole school approach will include a more caring ethos, a broader and more relevant curriculum, and a more sensitive school organisation.

In doing this, the contributors take as a starting point the Warnock Report of 1978 and the subsequent 1981 Education Act. They recognise that a cultivated awareness of special educational needs will bring about differences in teaching and management techniques which can be beneficial, not just for those children with learning difficulties, but for *all* children in our schools.

Both the Warnock Report and the 1981 Education Act succeeded, at least, in bringing about an awareness of the term 'special educational needs'. But it would be wrong to assume that awareness of the ideas contained therein was accompanied by enthusiasm in mainstream education. The dismay experienced by many mainstream teachers when the idea of integration was mooted, has been alleviated to some extent by the fact that in practice, many years after the Act, integration has been only patchily achieved, and has not resulted in large numbers of children being moved from special schools into ordinary schools.

But concern about this kind of integration – from special to ordinary schools – sometimes clouds the more general message which Warnock carried. The Warnock committee assumed that one in six children at any time, or one in five children at some time in their school career, will require some form of special help. It therefore assumed that it was fundamentally important to consider the special needs of children already in the mainstream. In abolishing categories of handicap and replacing them with the notion of special educational needs, the 1981 Act took up the Warnock theme in two ways:

1 It appreciated the fact that any child, of any level of ability, from any background, could at some time have some special need; and
2 It recognised that most children with special needs are already in mainstream education.

Since the passing of the 1981 Act there has been a developing awareness of the fact that there are indeed many children whose educational needs have, in the past, been ignored or neglected. This awareness has stretched to children across the spectrum of ability. The Act has enabled educationists to look for the reasons for the failure or underachievement of so many children.

It must be recognised, however, that a growing number of teachers and headteachers in the mainstream are experiencing a deep sense of unease over the Warnock recommendations. Many practitioners are worried that 'integrated' children will not fare well and they are often cynical about the reasons behind a policy of integration which sometimes appears to be muddle-headed and underfunded. Many feel ill-prepared for the changes that special needs staff are proposing within their own schools and suspect that a bandwagon is being jumped on. In short, many practitioners in the mainstream are suspicious about the motives behind changes in provision for special needs. They have every right to be suspicious. Major changes are being proposed in the way provision is made for special needs, often with very little thought or planning or in-service training. How are mainstream teachers to teach additional children – children often with quite serious problems – with no help other than a few hours welfare assistance a week? How are they to work alongside colleagues from the remedial department – colleagues who formerly withdrew difficult or slow-learning children to a separate room? And how are they to teach the other children in the class while all this is going on?

These are real and serious questions. They are not the knee-jerk reaction to change of the unconfident or unmotivated. They have to be addressed if the spirit of Warnock and the 1981 Act – a spirit with which most if not all would concur – are to be realised. For if they are not addressed, changes in the way special needs are met will surely fail, as other innovations in education have failed, through inadequate preparation, funding, in-service training and evaluation.

This book attempts to set these questions in context, by providing a framework for a whole school response to the challenge of meeting special needs. Geared primarily but not exclusively towards the secondary school, it suggests that special needs cannot effectively be met without the determined efforts of the whole school community. For it is in the larger, more complex environment of the secondary school that such coordinated efforts are most needed. In the primary school, communication is often much easier; one teacher takes prime responsibility for one class so the atmosphere is more child-centred, and there is less of a divide between academic areas and the pastoral and academic sides of school life. Many primary headteachers could justifiably claim that a whole school approach already operates in their schools.

The focus then is on the secondary area, where far greater problems are likely to be encountered in effecting coordination of this kind. The book begins by looking at the concept of a whole school approach and it proceeds by examining how the concept can be translated into practice through the management of the school and the organisation of the classroom. It then goes on to examine how teaching might be adapted for children of all abilities by looking at the way in which language – spoken, read and written – is used through the curriculum. As special needs in the mainstream are often synonymous with behaviour difficulties, a chapter is devoted entirely to the ways in which the school and the classroom can be organised to minimise such difficulties.

The emphasis throughout is preventive. The assumption is not that special needs reside in a particular group of children who have to be identified and then catered for. Rather, we assume that our education system has for decades seen children who have experienced difficulties removed to a special class or a special school; as such it has enabled the development of curricula and systems of organisation which take scant account of such children. Only through a reappraisal and a restructuring of those traditions, curricula and systems of organisation, will special needs be met appropriately in the mainstream. Our final chapter therefore takes account of the wider context in which these traditions have emerged and looks to the future for the youngsters currently in our charge in order that an appropriate curriculum can be framed for them. It proceeds by examining some of the wider implications for the school in terms of in-service education for effecting a whole school approach.

1
The Concept of a Whole School Approach to Special Needs

Caroline Roaf

This chapter is concerned with the development of attitudes, organisation and a curriculum consistent with an ethos in which children are valued equally and in which their rights are recognised. It is a tall order but one which may provide the key to the pressing problem of how to raise motivation and achievement, for all children regardless of sex, colour or class.

It involves exploring the implications of this in 'teacher-centred' terms – emphasising, in other words, that it is only possible to promote an essentially 'child-centred' ethos with teachers who have developed, in their training and practice, some understanding of what is implied by the principle of equal value, and what has to be done in terms of organisation and curriculum to ensure that this is happening. There is, however, a prior need and that is to find out what lies behind the term special educational needs; who are we talking about and why is a whole school approach so consistently advocated?

What is Meant by 'Special Educational Needs'?*

The Warnock Committee admitted having great difficulty in formulating the concept of special educational needs, from which the rest of us, who also experience difficulty with it, can

---

* This section is based on an article by Caroline Roaf which appeared in *The Times Educational Supplement* on 18 September, 1987.

take heart. They found it 'impossible to establish precise criteria for defining what constitutes handicap', found that 'the idea is deeply engrained in educational thinking that there are two types of children, the handicapped and the non-handicapped' and therefore they wished 'to see a more positive approach, and ... have adopted the concept of special educational needs, seen not in terms of a particular disability which a child may be judged to have, but in relation to everything about him, his abilities as well as his disabilities – indeed *all the factors which have a bearing on his educational progress*' [my italics] (DES, 1978).

It appears, then, that from the beginning there was a problem about exactly who was being referred to in the use of this term. The Fish Report (ILEA, 1985) makes a distinction between those with special educational needs (i.e. learning difficulties) and those with special needs (i.e. social and other needs). Whether or not this is a valid distinction is something I shall discuss later, but for the time being it is sufficient to note that the question of definition remains highly significant and problematic.

The 1981 Education Act, however, following the recommendation of the Warnock Report, abolished the categories of handicap. Children who had previously been described as belonging to any of these categories were described instead as having special educational needs. Thus the term was firmly associated with the notion of handicap, despite the intentions of the Report. And so it has remained, in practice and in much of the special needs literature, as a hidden, or not so hidden, assumption that children with special needs have learning difficulties which arise from defects *in themselves*. Therefore, we have a situation in which large numbers of children, in spite of the fact that handicapped people have never constituted more than a tiny percentage of society, are regarded as having special needs which are then attributed to learning difficulty and, by implication, to handicap. It is a telling indication of the extent of the prejudice still existing against any form of handicap, that this remains a highly stigmatising and fear-laden association. But even if it were not, overemphasising the association of special needs with learning difficulties would be misleading, since it encourages a child-centred stance which locates the problem in the child, rather than in the surrounding attitudes and environment: an environment in which racism, sexism, classism, and ageism, to say nothing of poor housing and health conditions, conspire together to limit children's opportunities and teachers' expectations of them. Up and down the country there are teachers working to promote equal opportunities, even whole schools, who recognise this. They know that a child-centred awareness of individual needs and rights has to be balanced by a teacher-centred awareness of prejudice and unfair discrimination in the structures of school and society. Whole school approaches to meet special needs of children are therefore essentially about rights and justice. It becomes a question of being able to analyse what these rights are and of finding a new language with which to do it.

The Warnock Report itself was based on the realisation that the degree to which people are handicapped by physical or mental disability, and the ease or difficulty with which they can be integrated into the community, depends to a large extent on community attitudes and prejudices. The relative nature of handicap has been increasingly appreciated because disabled people themselves, and others who have fought with them for their rights, have supported investment in the research and resources needed to assert those rights. One only has to look at the number of ramps now leading into buildings, at the adaptation of pavements to help wheelchairs at road crossings, to realise that some awareness of this, however limited, has penetrated the civic mind and purse. Similarly, in many schools, the move towards integration is a genuine one at both the level of staffing, and resources (large-type typewriters, wheelchair hoists on staircases, deaf-aid loops) and of attitudes in which it is recognised that:

> a framework is needed within which children may use *as of right* the general facilities available at school and also receive the special help that they require (DES, 1978).

Detaching the concept of special needs from its origins in handicap, and rooting it instead in human rights, allows us to do two things: it frees us from a child-centred obsession with individual learning difficulties and it allows us to accept the reality that children are frequently the victims of a combination of different kinds of prejudice and discrimination. For instance, some black, working-class girls have special needs but none of them will be met by a 'difference blind' approach rooted in learning difficulties. How then, in this view of special educational needs, do we place the work of the teacher responsible for meeting special needs, and what is now implied by the notion of a whole school approach?

What is Meant by Whole School Policy?

The history and development of the phrase 'whole school policy' sheds some light, from an independent source, on the question of special needs and tends to support the view that special needs is as much a question of rights as of needs. We must first, however, establish a working definition of whole school policy and then, by looking at some topics currently the subject of whole school policy making, find the common issues they share.

Whole school policy has been the subject of remarkably little study as a concept in its own right, in spite of the fact that it has been increasingly used since the publication of the Bullock Report (DES, 1975). The idea, in that report, of 'language across the curriculum' later taken up by Marland (1977), seems to have established the phrase as a useful one, but one which has been associated almost exclusively with particular topics such as language, special needs or multicultural education. This has tended to obscure any links or common issues which there might be between one whole school policy and another. The first article to appear which asked questions about whole school policy as a generic term was in 1985 (Boyd). This was followed by an article in 1986 (Roaf), in which the following definition of whole school policy was suggested:

> A policy clearly understood by the whole school community whose purpose is to guide and determine the ethos of the school and to support attitudes and behaviour consistent with that ethos.

It is clear from a definition such as this that many different kinds of school policy could be referred to in it, and that many different kinds of school ethos could be embraced by it. Schools with pronounced views on, for example, corporal punishment, single-sex education, or a particular theory of evolution, or schools founded on a particular educational philosophy or religion, would be likely to have whole school policies whose purpose was to guide and determine an ethos consistent with that philosophy. For the present purpose, the ethos in question is that of the maintained comprehensive school (covering all age groups) in which children are to be educated to their full potential in an environment in which they are valued equally. It means, significantly, the development of an ethos which faces the challenge of being required to reconcile an educational philosophy with a social philosophy. Within that context, it further becomes clear that while many policies are 'whole school' (uniform, discipline), it is only some which are singled out for special 'whole school' treatment.

If we look at three of these, special educational needs, multicultural education and gender, some interesting points emerge. All three have two kinds of activity in common. The first is a concern with society's attitude and behaviour towards specific groups of children, emphasising questions of prejudice and discrimination about which society as a whole should be aware

> Such an outcome [integration] will not occur spontaneously. Nor will it be achieved by legislation alone. It has to be contrived and patiently nurtured. It means greater discrimination in favour of those children with special needs, in proportion to the severity of their disabilities (DES, 1978).

The second is a concern to examine the needs of specific groups of children; their needs as individuals, and their needs as members of identifiable groups. The Swann Report (DES, 1985) recognised that some ethnic minority pupils:

> have certain educational needs which may call for particular responses from schools. As the debate on multicultural education has increasingly come to focus on the broader aspects of provision for all pupils, the development of appropriate policies to respond to the particular educational needs which ethnic minority pupils may experience has tended to be subsumed within this broader context rather than analysed in any depth . . . it is also essential that the education system caters for any specific educational needs which these pupils may experience, in order to offer them the true equality of opportunity which we have advocated.

Turning then to the question of gender, the Equal Opportunities Commission suggest that:

> Educational provision should be so planned that the staffing and physical resources are sufficient to provide the type, range and level of subjects required, so as to ensure that equally favourable opportunities are available to pupils of both sexes with common aptitudes, needs and desires, so that equality of opportunity is seen to be a reality

for both sexes. This may mean a gradual alteration in the distribution of resources (EOC, 1985).

What seems to emerge, therefore, is that in viewing certain whole school policies as concerned with human rights, we find a balance being sought between general attitudinal change and the provision of particular physical resources. In gender and race the stress has tended to be on attitude, while in handicap it has been on resources. A human rights perspective on the issue of handicap thus reaffirms and emphasises the importance of attitude change. For the mentally handicapped some might think this emphasis is one which is long overdue.

This analysis draws attention to two important points. The first is that in any typology of whole school policy there would appear to be one group which is concerned with human rights. The second is that needs arise, though not exclusively, where there are violations of rights. We therefore find ourselves able to draw a few conclusions on the subject of whole school approaches. Policy, according to dictionary definition is:

– 'any course of action adopted as advantageous or expedient'

– 'a definite course of action selected among many alternatives, to guide and determine future decisions.'

It is perhaps no coincidence that for very many reasons the rise of the comprehensive school, itself a symptom of societal change, has been accompanied by a rising interest in, and concern for, human rights. Typically these occur in the sphere of gender, race, handicap and class and also, in relation to global issues, a concern with, for example, the distribution of resources. Whole school policies have emerged out of this concern, sometimes simply because they are seen as 'advantageous or expedient'. In many, however, they have been seen as a genuine response to the comprehensive principle of equal value and as a way of giving practical expression to what would otherwise simply be an abstraction.

We can conclude therefore that among whole school policies or approaches, there are some which we may regard as human rights policies, which usually address some issue of current concern, and whose purpose is to work towards goals which will, when achieved, become part of the school's ethos and that the creation of this ethos will enable schools to analyse their needs with greater accuracy and help them to push for the resources and other changes they need in order to meet them. They will then stand a greater chance of being able to create an environment in which needs do not arise in the first place.

Learning Difficulty and Special Provision

Thus Warnock's often quoted 'broader and more positive' view of special education: 'it encompasses the whole range and variety of additional help, wherever it is provided . . . by which children may be helped to overcome educational difficulties, however they are caused' takes on a new meaning. Having released the concept of special needs from its association solely with handicap, we can accept the complexity of the term 'educational' or 'learning' difficulties and acknowledge that children's needs have many different and overlapping causes, which will be best met by an understanding and assertion of their rights. In re-assessing the Warnock Report we can likewise begin to re-examine the 1981 Act. Section 1.4, for example, states that:

> A child is not to be taken as having a learning difficulty solely because the language (or form of the language) in which he [sic] is, or will be, taught is different from a language (or form of a language) which has at any time been spoken in his home.

Although strangely worded, this section does make the very important distinction between children who need special provision and have learning difficulties, and those who do not have learning difficulties but for whom special provision may nonetheless be required. Unfortunately the wording of the Act, and the political climate of the time, was such that this section was taken to refer only to ethnic minority children whose first language was not English. Those who did not teach such children simply dismissed the section as irrelevant to them. This was a pity since, in fact, the reality is rather different. Large numbers of children are taught in a form of language which differs from that spoken at home. In many, even most, areas, the formal language of education is very different from the language of home, and for how many children is the language question unconnected with other factors such as class? Even for those children who enter school speaking a language other than English and who indisputably need teaching in English as a second language, the more these children are the victims of class and race prejudice and discrimination, the more they are disadvantaged and have their chances of success reduced. Thus, there can be very few children for whom it can be truly said that they have 'learning difficulties' within the meaning of the Act. It is this too, which makes the Fish distinction between 'special needs' and 'special *educational* needs' very difficult to sustain.

This does not, of course, prevent children in school from presenting to their teachers *as if* they had learning difficulties. It will be asked in that case, does this distinction matter? If they appear to have learning difficulties, is this not sufficient reason to treat them as if they had? This has in fact been the pragmatic approach of many teachers to date, and although it has had its successes it has also not been without its critics.

I have already discussed in principle the problems inherent in the view of special needs which sees it in terms of learning difficulties rather than in terms of rights. I will now briefly discuss this in terms of the type of special provision which is required to meet needs arising from prejudice and unfair discrimination, or, put another way, from violations of rights, rather than from learning difficulties. It will be argued that it is in the analysis of these and the development of strategies to remove them that special needs are most likely to be met successfully and further, that this should be at the heart of the job for teachers concerned with special needs, providing the rationale for many of the changes of emphasis in the ways in which they are currently being encouraged to work.

From this perspective it will be seen that just as whole school approaches to special needs are about rights and a school's responsibilities towards all its students in addressing these issues, so teachers with special responsibility for meeting students' needs will be concerned with the implementation of human rights policies. The moves towards mixed-ability grouping and teaching, and towards the integration into mainstream of pupils previously in special schools, were fought for by those who were interested primarily in children's rights. Similarly, the allocation of funding for those whose first language is not English has been seen as both a need and a right, and questions concerning the development of community and mother tongue languages have been conducted very markedly in terms of rights. Gender issues are similarly seen as a question of rights.

Children themselves are, in general, usually conscious of the occasions on which they feel the effects of prejudice and unfair discrimination and tend to respond in ways frequently described by teachers as lacking in motivation, being aggressive, or more generally simply as underachieving. For many teachers it confirms a view of certain types of children for whom expectations are simply 'low'. This is not to say that children do not behave in ways such as those described above for entirely different reasons, but simply to point out that there is an important distinction to be made.

In such a context, the traditional focus of special provision on basic skills is still important and emphatically part of a child's right. However, it will be addressed in a manner which sees that lack of success with such skills is as likely to be caused by lack of motivation stemming from some form of injustice, as from inherent learning difficulty or laziness. How many teachers have noticed that children's handwriting, presentation, spelling and other basic skills improve dramatically when they are convinced of their own worth, the importance of what they are doing and the teacher's determination to value their efforts and encourage them?

It would be grossly unfair to suggest that the importance of positive attitudes has not been recognised by many teachers. It has, and it has also received recognition in countless initiatives, such as criterion as opposed to norm referencing in tests and examinations, records of achievement and so on, at national, LEA and school level. But it would also be true to say that there is still a long way to go in terms of attracting the resources and staffing ratios required to counteract the effect of generations of discrimination and disadvantage. It also has to be said that unless teachers with responsibility for meeting special needs see themselves, and are recognised by their schools, as being an important mechanism for making special provision in *whatever* circumstances children find themselves discriminated against, they are unlikely to realise their objective, which is to help all children achieve their full potential. For most schools this is an objective which is still a long way off and one which can only be reached by examining the implications for school management and the curriculum of a human rights perspective.

Implications for Management and the Curriculum

1   Socio-economic factors

If special needs arise from violations of rights, the implication is that we need to look at what these may be in any particular set of circumstances and observe how they interact. Teachers will need to become much more aware than hitherto of the socio-economic and ethnic composition of their schools and the communities they serve. They will need to undertake target group studies from time to time, to ensure for example, that all activities are open to boys and girls alike, or that grouping, banding or setting arrangements do not lead to inequalities between different ethnic or cultural groups and to scrutinise the criteria used to determine pupil groupings and entry to certain courses. Schools with high proportions of children from minority groups, including those whose first language is not English, are frequently in the forefront here in their attempts to meet the needs of their pupils by their insistence on anti-racism and the development of a curriculum appropriate to life in a multicultural society. These schools recognise, for example, the rights of all their pupils to observe religious festivals, customs relating to dress or diet and to be taught the language of their communities. Likewise, schools with positive integration policies and close links with neighbouring special schools have done much to modify their curriculum and resources in ways which will make integration a reality.

2   The vehicles of prejudice

Unfair discrimination in schools is unlikely to be reduced without some understanding of the way in which prejudice arises and is perpetuated. We have already observed, for example, the powerful effect on the concept of special needs, of prejudice against any form of handicap.

(a)   In institutions

Institutional prejudice can result in indirect discrimination; that is, procedures, rules and criteria (age limits, the criteria for entry to certain courses) can have discriminatory effects which they were not originally intended to have. When deciding norms and criteria, whom, for example, do we have in mind? The able bodied? The literate? Those whose first language is English? Some students' needs may arise, therefore, not so much from learning difficulties or from inadequate staffing and resources, or even from inappropriate teaching methods and styles, as from undetected expressions of prejudice in the structure and organisation of the institution itself.

(b) In language and images

The fact that prejudice is so often perpetuated through language, visual images and customs, should alert us to the risks we take by not being sufficiently aware of their power. Our use of the words 'special needs' and the difficulty in overcoming the prejudice which associates with it terms such as 'cabbage' and 'flid' is perhaps sufficient warning. 'What are you doing in this class?', one teacher was overheard to say to a pupil, 'I thought you were better than that!'

3 Discrimination

Understanding the differences between fair and unfair discrimination must be one of the most difficult tasks for any teacher. It is one which is of particular importance to teachers responsible for meeting special needs because so often it is they who make critical decisions concerning special provisions and the allocation of scarce resources. Children have many different needs, and they cannot be treated as if they were all the same. The important question to ask is which differences are relevant and which are not in a given situation: making distinctions based on irrelevant differences can be as unjust as the failure to make distinctions based on relevant differences. On the basis of this, might track suits be allowed instead of shorts for PE, where the latter would give offence to Muslims, for example, or 'enrichment' materials be used in class, or vegetarian dishes appear on the school dinner menu? What are the implications, in terms of attitudes and resources, of accommodating a musically or mathematically gifted child or a child who is hard of hearing?

We have little trouble, for example, in accepting the idea that there should be separate toilets and changing rooms for boys and girls and that some children should have free meals and bus passes. We have been less ready to accept the need for other forms of special provision based on relevant differences of the kind suggested above, or even to notice that they might be necessary. Even when such differences and the provision required have been noticed, it has been very difficult to persuade those who control the purse strings that alterations to the buildings, resources and the curriculum, to say nothing of language and attitudes, are necessary.

It is no coincidence, then, that as human rights issues have risen in importance so has the scope and role of the teacher responsible for meeting special needs. The National Association for Remedial Education (NARE, 1985) considers the role to have seven broad features – assessment, prescriptive, liaison, management, staff development, teaching and support – which taken together place them at the very centre of school management and curriculum development. In schools which place a heavy emphasis on human rights issues, this is what one would expect. Policies which dispel prejudice and unfair discrimination give expression to the principle of equal value, and in putting these policies into effect, staff with the responsibility of meeting special needs can be of central importance and would be even more so if they were more explicit about this.

4   The whole school approach

What, then, would one expect of a school in which an interactive human rights view of special needs was understood? A checklist to identify the extent to which a whole school approach could be said to be in operation would be a good starting point. One would expect such a checklist to investigate the matter in three main areas.

(a)   The school itself, its ethos, structures and curriculum

– Is there a policy-making group which will take decisions on matters closely connected with the expression of the equal value principle, for example, the development of human rights policies, the formation of teaching/tutorial groups, the development of close community links? How are the decisions of this group filtered through to curriculum and pastoral structures? What about the physical structure of buildings and classrooms?
– Are there policies to promote knowledge and understanding of the way in which prejudice is perpetuated and how to minimise its effects in the specific areas of class, race, gender, handicap and age? How does the school ensure that these policies are implemented? Is this included in job descriptions or are there specific post holders? Are these issues tackled within the curriculum?

– How do the staff with responsibility for special needs operate and how do they understand their role?
– Are opportunities made for every pupil to experience success and achievement?
– Is there a system of curricular and pastoral support to meet the individual needs of staff and students?
– Does the curriculum itself convey parity of esteem between its different courses?

(b)   The needs and rights of the students within the school

– How does the school ensure that it meets the needs of all its pupils and how does it identify which groups of students or individuals these are? Excellence at sport or music, for example, is often an opportunity for pupils to be given extra tuition or time. Does this happen for those who excel in other areas?
– Is sufficient time given to counselling all students by a personal tutor and do these tutors have the support of other staff with whom they can discuss some of the issues we have outlined concerning relevant differences? To what extent have the timetable and group size implications of this been thought through?
– Are courses being developed, such as those characteristic of much outdoor and residential education, in which problem solving skills and collaborative group work, in sometimes unfamiliar situations, hold up, as it were, a mirror in which children may see themselves anew? Those who have taken part in such activities will not easily forget the sight of children, previously seen by their class mates as unsuccessful, suddenly gaining new feelings of success, confidence, and trust in others. A school in which the equal value principle is central to its ethos will insist that its students spend much of their time in circumstances in which this is an actual experience and in which they can become aware, in that spirit, of themselves both in relation to others and to their environment.

(c)   Home/school liaison and community links

– Does the school actively seek ways in which to serve the whole community and how close are its links with parents and other members of this wider school community?

- Does the school serve the community outside school hours?
- How responsive is the school to the views of parents and local employers?
- How close is the liaison with other educational establishments in the area, for example, special schools or units, youth clubs etc?

Summary and Conclusions

We have come a long way since the pre-Warnock view of special needs, rooted in handicap and obsessed with learning difficulties. While not denying that children will continue to need help in all the traditional ways, a whole school, human rights perspective allows us to look more widely for ways in which both to meet needs and to reduce their incidence and significance. In moving from the role of 'remedial' teacher working with the 'least able' in a segregative manner, to that of 'support' teacher working alongside mainstream colleagues, there has been a major shift in attitude. However, John Visser (1986), writing on the notion of support, comments:

> the term 'support' has drawbacks . . . it is advantageous as a descriptor of a teacher's work or role, especially as it reflects a move away from the child as the central and only focus of their professional duties.

Thus needs are seen as arising as much from surrounding attitudes and environment as from within children themselves. Continuing, he considers the drawbacks in the use of the term 'support' to be that so much of the teacher's role 'has an active, dynamic quality to it' which the notion of support belies. A perspective, therefore, which emphasises human rights, offers teachers a way of escaping the effect of that historical foundation of special needs in handicap, of reaching out to the much more complex needs of their students, and of finding a new dynamic for their work.

References

BOYD, B. (1985) 'Whole school policies', *Forum for the Discussion of New Trends in Education, 27*, 3, 5.

DEPARTMENT OF EDUCATION AND SCIENCE (1975) *A Language for Life* (Bullock Report). London: HMSO.
DEPARTMENT OF EDUCATION AND SCIENCE (1978) *Special Educational Needs* (Warnock Report). London: HMSO.
DEPARTMENT OF EDUCATION AND SCIENCE (1985) *Education for All* (Swann Report). London: HMSO.
EQUAL OPPORTUNITIES COMMISSION (1985) *Do You Provide Equal Educational Opportunities?* (p.18). Manchester: EOC.
INNER LONDON EDUCATION AUTHORITY (1985) *Educational Opportunities for All?* (Fish Report). London: ILEA.
MARLAND, M. (1977) *Language Across the Curriculum*. London: Heinemann Educational Books.
NATIONAL ASSOCIATION FOR REMEDIAL EDUCATION (1985) *Teaching Roles for Special Educational Needs*, Guidelines 6. Stafford: NARE.
ROAF, C. (1986) 'Whole school policy: principles and practice', *Forum for the Discussion of New Trends in Education*, 29, 1, 20.
VISSER, J (1986) 'Support: a description of the work of the SEN professional', *Support for Learning*, 1, 4, 79.

2
Organisation for a Whole School Approach

John Howson

Introducing any change into a school can be a difficult and uncertain process, not only for those who are initiating the change, but also for the rest of the staff and for anyone else concerned with the school. Unless the change is introduced in a positive way, many members of staff will feel threatened and may react in a negative manner. In view of the fact that any change, whether for better or worse, is likely to result in a period of discomfort for the participants, this is not perhaps a surprising reaction. This chapter will explore some of the difficulties which may be encountered by those involved in initiating a change, such as the introduction of a whole school approach to children with special needs. By being aware of these difficulties it is to be hoped that the possibilities of introducing a successful change will be increased.

The Changing Education Environment

Until recently education operated virtually in isolation from the rest of society. Schools were generally regarded as uncomplicated institutions, pursuing clearcut goals based around an agreed view of what was meant by education. The view of education as 'unproblematic' applied both to those working in schools and to many of those concerned with policy making in education. In the past twenty years all this has changed and it is in middle and secondary schools that the changes have probably been felt most. On one level there have been organisational changes, such as the introduction of new structures including middle schools, sixth form colleges, tertiary colleges and community colleges, and on a different level there have been considerable changes within schools as the new structures have evolved.

There have been fewer organisational changes at primary level, but many schools in this area have begun to develop their particular organisational structures by including facilities for pre-school children through nursery classes. There is also a growing trend towards providing support for mothers with even younger children.

Another important area of change which has affected the way in which schools are managed, has been the introduction of non-selective secondary education. One effect of the introduction of comprehensive schools was that, in general, secondary schools became larger. The HMI Secondary School Survey (1979) showed that comprehensive schools are larger than other types of schools. Comprehensive schools averaged about 1000 pupils whereas grammar and secondary modern schools averaged about 600, with only a few instances of schools of either type exceeding 1000 pupils. Despite the decline in pupil numbers since the end of the 1970s as a result of demographic changes, there is no reason to believe that there has been any significant shift in policy towards making comprehensive schools smaller.

In addition to changes in organisation and size, there is a third area of change in schools which has probably had even more far-reaching effects. This has been the demise of the relative isolation of education from the rest of society. In the early 1970s legislation on employment law, health and safety, equal opportunities and race relations brought schools within the framework of a whole set of new legislation concerned with employees' working lives for the first time. An even bigger change occurred when politicians and others outside the education system began to take an interest in what happened in schools. The milestone which charts this change was the speech which Prime Minister James Callaghan gave at Ruskin College in Oxford in late 1976. One outcome of this speech was the launch of the 'Great Debate' about education which culminated in the 1977 Green Paper (DES, 1977). The pace of change has never let up since.

At the same time during the 1970s as politicians and others were taking an interest in education, there were also a number of important committees considering various aspects of education. The effects of the Taylor (1977), Warnock (1978) and more recently the Swann (1985) Committees have also had profound effects on many schools. All these influences have caused

schools to undergo a whole series of changes in a wide range
of areas. The effects of the 1986 Education Act only began to
be felt in schools in 1987 and now schools of all types have to
produce an annual report which is open to scrutiny by parents
at an annual meeting. Changes in the composition of governing
bodies reduce further the control local politicians can exercise
over individual schools. Schools are becoming more aware
of their reputation in the local community, and soon the
era of the school isolated from its community will be at an end.

All these developments mean that any school attempting
change will need to do everything possible to ensure that the
change is a success. Therefore, there will have to be a clear plan
which will provide the focus for the introduction of the change.
This is not an easy process, for as Paisey (1982) has written,
'innovation [is] a complex and difficult process'; to be successful
it will require the application of many different skills.

Factors Involved in Change

Before any change is implemented, those involved need to
consider the situation in which the change will take place.
Unless the possible effects are considered, then there is a
strong risk that some vital factor will be forgotten and all
the planning will be wasted. To ignore the planning stage
completely when undertaking any change, is to take the risk
that 'it will be all right on the night'; of course it never is.

There are four main areas which need to be considered
when contemplating changes in a school which are likely to
affect a number of people. These are time, people, space,
and materials. All four areas are equally important and do
not, of course, operate in isolation from each other.

Time

In some models of change, such as that by Bolam (1975),
time is used as the frame of reference for understanding the
change process. This can be a useful approach and is one that
is familiar to many teachers. Bolam divided the change process
into three stages: before, during and after the change has taken
place. At each stage there are different considerations. During
the first stage the change is planned, during the second the
change is introduced and during the third the change is

evaluated. Subsequent to the evaluation there may be a period of modification before it is fully adopted into the operating system of the school. It then becomes subject to whatever pattern of scrutiny exists within the school for monitoring existing structures, since it is then no longer a change. Too many schools still lack this regular appraisal of existing systems resulting in something happening 'because it has always been done that way'.

The time spent on planning the introduction of any change is never wasted, and can be used to produce a timetable for change which will also help to identify any likely problems before they arise. This does not mean necessarily that all problems will be spotted before they occur – just that some of the more obvious ones will be taken into consideration. This will leave more time and energy to cope with the unexpected problems when they do arise.

There is another aspect to the time angle which needs to be considered. This is the extent to which change carries implications for the use of staff time and if so, where that time is going to come from. If, for example, the introduction of a whole school approach to special needs means that a teacher is designated as a consultant, then to undertake the task properly the teacher will need both time to learn the skills associated with the new role, and also time to perform the task in the future. Failure to provide for this will mean that either one set of tasks is ignored or else both the existing role and the new task are performed badly, with a consequent loss of effectiveness on the part of the teacher.

People

Anyone contemplating introducing change into a school needs to be aware that such a move will involve the cooperation of a great many people if it is to be a success. For many schools the move to a whole school approach to special needs will be a major upheaval in the life of the school and will therefore affect a great many people, both directly and indirectly. The stage at which individuals within the school, and associated with the school, need to become involved with any change is up to each individual school. To some extent, it will depend upon factors such as where the desire for change originated and the history of change in the school. Schools consist of two types of staff: professionals – that is the teachers – and support staff – that is all the other people who work in the school. Both groups may be affected by change and commonsense dictates that they should be consulted about how the change will be introduced.

Insiders

During the 1980s there has been a great deal written about the management of schools (for example, Everard and Morris, 1986; Hughes, 1985; Marland, 1986). There has been a trend in some cases to view management from an industrial perspective. This has been reinforced by the political climate of the 1980s with its emphasis on the market economy. Schools have been seen by some as hierachical institutions presided over by headteachers who are increasingly expected to perform managerial roles while classroom teachers are seen to occupy some lower level in the hierachy.

There is, however, a school of thought which suggests that education is different from industry because it lacks the profit motive. It can be argued that education is closer to the professions in that it offers a service where all the professionals have a part to play in helping the institution reach its goal. Teachers, as professionals, are responsible for ensuring that children in school receive the most appropriate education for their needs and, as such, have a right to be involved in changes which affect their working lives. Indeed, a new policy is unlikely to be successful unless the staff have been convinced that it is the right decision and however much either a headteacher or a group of enthusiasts are committed to the introduction of a change which affects the working lives of other staff it is unlikely to succeed if the remainder of the staff do not appreciate its value. This is a particular problem when staff have to adopt new functions. The introduction of a whole school approach to special needs may well provide for one teacher to act in the role of consultant to other members of staff. In primary schools the role of consultant has been gaining ground as teachers have realised that they no longer have the expertise to cover developments in all subjects. An additional consultant is, therefore, no novelty even if in this instance the post would relate to how children with special needs are provided for in the ordinary classroom rather than to a particular curriculum area.

In many secondary schools the position may be rather different. The typical organisational pattern of comprehensive schools has produced a structure which has tended to compartmentalise various functions into either dealing with individual academic areas or specific groups of children, such as year groups. Very few teachers below the senior management rank have what might be described as a service function offering advice to the whole staff. Traditional special needs departments have usually operated on the basis of removing children from mainstream classes either for particular lessons or for significant periods of time. A whole school approach will mean that many more teachers will come into contact with children who have special needs. These teachers will need to be able to turn to someone within the school for help and advice in dealing with the problems they are faced with, in teaching children for whom normal teaching methods are not always appropriate.

Outsiders

An important change which was first introduced during 1987 was the increased powers given to governing bodies under the 1986 Education Act. Governing bodies now have much greater access to decision making than ever before, even in areas from which they have hitherto been excluded, such as the curriculum. By implication, this could mean that governors can discuss not only what is taught but also the manner in which it is taught. There is a clear difficulty here between the role of the professional expert, as represented by the headteacher and the staff of the school, and the layperson's knowledge and perceptions as represented by most governing bodies. The extent to which governing bodies will use these powers is still unknown. It may be that the weakening of political control of governing bodies resulting from the change in composition introduced by the 1986 Education Act will strengthen the hand of the headteacher. However, an alternative outcome might be an increase in the involvement of governing bodies in the running of schools as more governors have responsibility for just one individual school.

To some extent governing bodies, like headteachers, are likely to develop an attitude to change which is affected increasingly by their view of how the school stands in the market place – a view which is unlikely to be publicly expressed. However, if schools, at least in urban areas, are made to be more competitive, then changes will in many cases be viewed against how they affect this competitive position. Heads and governing bodies may be even more nervous of rocking the boat, even for sound educational reasons, unless they can feel secure that it will not reduce the number of parents seeking places for children at the school. To this extent primary schools are generally in a more secure position than secondary schools.

The 1986 Education Act gave parents a direct say in the running of schools through the establishment of annual school meetings. These were first held during 1987 and were clearly intended by the government as a means by which parents could express their views about the way a school was being run, and if necessary pass resolutions requesting change. The evidence available from a sample of schools after the first round of meetings (Davies, Holmes *et al*, 1987) suggests that, at least in the schools studied, the meetings had little or no effect on school policy.

Whether this will always be the situation is an open question. What is certain, is that now the consumer has a statutory voice in the education process, then it may well be more difficult in the future for headteachers to ignore them when considering introducing any change into a school. The need to explain to parents the reasons behind the introduction of a new policy, has become vital now that parents have this formal procedure by which they can question the way a school is functioning. It will only need a few parents to misunderstand the reasons for a change and convince themselves that it is detrimental to their own children's education for headteachers to be faced with a difficult challenge at an annual school meeting. Fortunately for headteachers, those who formulated the provisions for annual meetings for schools did not provide for the possibility of parents being able to call a special meeting, as for instance shareholders have the right to do under the Companies Act. Thus the meeting can be kept firmly in the hands of the chairman of the governors and the headteacher.

Space

Any change is likely to involve space considerations. The introduction of a whole school policy on special needs is no exception. Unfortunately, schools are generally inflexible as regards the use of space. However, any need to alter teaching practices as a result of a change in policy, should produce a complementary review of classroom organisation, and the opportunity should be taken to review the existing list of outstanding building and capital items on the school's shopping list as it may well be that new requirements will have emerged from a change.

Materials

Most schools are seriously under-resourced but this is not a new situation and evidence would suggest that the problem has been growing worse over the past few years (HMI, 1987). This shortage of resources has developed because schools are labour-intensive institutions, and are required to provide education for all children between the ages of five and sixteen. Thus, when resources are no longer in unlimited supply, it is likely that the lack of growth will be most keenly felt in areas other than in the number of teachers in schools. This does not mean that teaching resources are evenly divided within schools, between schools or even between local authorities. A glance at any table of pupil-teacher ratios (see for instance DES Statistical Bulletin 6/86) will show the wide range between the best and worst authorities which government-subsidised market economy policies have produced over the period since the end of the the old quota system. This free market system subsidised by the rate support grant has generally worked to the detriment of the naturally conservative shire counties.

Of course not all teachers employed by local authorities teach in schools and the growing number of support, advisory and other non-school based teachers only serve to complicate the position. The net result is, however, that a wider range of staffing levels probably exists across England now than at any other time since the passing of the 1944 Education Act. The implication of this position is that in some authorities, it will be much easier to obtain help and support for the development of any new policy. At least special needs is an area which the DES has accorded a high level of priority in terms of in-service training under the arrangements which came into force in 1987.

How then can headteachers acquire the extra resources necessary to implement a new policy? Various strategies can be suggested. The most obvious includes a reorganisation of existing arrangements, although financially the possibility of this is unlikely without depriving existing programmes of support. Indeed, in those schools where expenditure decisions are arrived at only after a period of discussion, the problem is even more acute. The obvious alternative is to seek new sources of finance. In the present climate this usually means asking parents and friends of the school for support. While this is an obvious short-term solution, various problems arise when tying long-term projects to this sort of finance – the most obvious being that this method of financing is potentially unpredictable. For that reason, it is best used for 'extras' rather than for financing anything which is to be a continuing feature of school life.

As special needs has been identified as a priority area by the DES in terms of in-service training, it may be that schools will be able to obtain help from their local authorities for an introduction of a whole school approach. Again, the problem is likely to be that although money may be available to start the change, future financing will need to come from ordinary running costs. This dilemma of funding change is not unique to the area of special needs, many schools have faced the same problem in relation to microcomputers where money was made available to establish projects, but the funding for continuing the project in future years was left to the schools' own initiatives.

Successfully Introducing the Change

It is important to remember that at every step in a change, it is *people* who will have the greatest influence on what happens, and in particular the person who instigates the change. In many books this person is called the 'change agent'. It is how this person handles the change which will determine just how successful it will be. A great deal will depend upon the personal qualities of the change agent, and whether the rest of the staff respect his/her ideas. They will also need to be enthusiastic and convincing about what they want to happen in order to sell their ideas and have the managerial skills to involve and motivate other people. Everard and Morris (1986) provide a list of such qualities for successful managers of change, which is reproduced below.

QUALITIES FOR 'MANAGERS OF CHANGE'

Knowledge of

1 People and their motivational systems – what makes them tick.
2 Organisations as social systems – what makes them healthy and effective and able to achieve objectives.
3 The environment surrounding the organisation – the systems that impinge on it and make demands of it.
4 Managerial styles and their effects on work.
5 One's own personal managerial style and proclivities.

6 Organisational processes such as decision making, planning, control, communications, conflict management and reward systems.
7 The process of change.
8 Educational training methods and theory.

KNOWLEDGE REQUIRED FOR MANAGING CHANGE

Skills in

1 Analysing large complex systems.
2 Collecting and processing large amounts of information and simplifying it for action.
3 Goal-setting and planning.
4 Getting consensus decisions.
5 Conflict management.
6 Empathy.
7 Political behaviour.
8 Public relations.
9 Consulting and counselling.
10 Training and teaching.

SKILLS REQUIRED FOR MANAGING CHANGE

1 A strong sense of personal ethics which helps to ensure consistent behaviour.
2 Something of an intellectual by both training and temperament.
3 A strong penchant towards optimism.
4 Enjoyment of the intrinsic rewards of effectiveness, without the need for public approval.
5 High willingness to take calculated risks and live with the consequences without experiencing undue stress.
6 A capacity to accept conflict and enjoy managing it.
7 A soft voice and low-key manner.
8 A high degree of self-awareness – knowledge of self.
9 A high tolerance of ambiguity and complexity.
10 A tendency to avoid polarizing issues into black and white, right and wrong.
11 High ability to listen.

Reproduced from *School Organisation*, Everard, K. and Morris, G. (1986) Harper and Row

The present climate in schools is more concerned with a move towards a cooperative style of decision making rather than one where an authoritarian headteacher imposes change on the staff. This more open style of decision making can only work where there is a recognition of the need for continuous staff development. Once teachers have been encouraged to take part in the policy making decisions of the school, then they are unlikely to adopt passive roles in future policy making.

Conclusion

To bring about a change in schools requires careful planning and skilful management. The change will need to pass through a series of stages before it becomes incorporated into the lifestyle of the school. All members of the school organisation involved with, or affected by, the change need to be kept up to date on what is happening and careful evaluation and assessment need to take place at all stages. Above all, it is the people in the school who are the ones who can make a success or failure of a change. If care is taken by those designing the change to involve people and remove fears of the unknown by keeping high standards of communication, then there should be every expectation that the change will be successfully implemented.

References

AUDIT COMMISSION (1986) *Towards Better Management of Secondary Education.* London: HMSO.
BOLAM, R. (1975) 'The management of educational change: towards a conceptual framework', in HOUGHTON, V., McHUGH, R. and MORGAN, C. (eds) *Management in Education.* London: Ward Lock Educational.
DAVIES, J., HOLMES, G, HOWSON, S.O. and ORMSTON, M. (1987) 'Survey of school meetings', *Independent*, 20 July 1987 p.2 and leader comment.
DEPARTMENT OF EDUCATION AND SCIENCE (1977) *Education in Schools a Consultative Document* CMND 6869. London: HMSO.
DEPARTMENT OF EDUCATION AND SCIENCE (1977) *A New Partnership for our Schools* (Taylor Report). London: HMSO.
DEPARTMENT OF EDUCATION AND SCIENCE (1978) *Special Educational Needs* (Warnock Report). London: HMSO.
DEPARTMENT OF EDUCATION AND SCIENCE (1985) *Education for All* (Swann Report). London: HMSO.

DEPARTMENT OF EDUCATION AND SCIENCE (1986) Statistical Bulletin No. 6/86 *Pupil Teacher Ratios for Each Local Authority in England – January 1985*. London: DES.

EVERARD, K. and MORRIS, G. 1986) *School Organisation*. London: Harper and Row.

HER MAJESTY'S INSPECTORATE (1979) *Secondary School Survey*. London: HMSO.

HER MAJESTY'S INSPECTORATE (1987) *Report by HMI on the Effects of Local Authority Expenditure Policies on Education Provision in England – 1986*. London: DES.

HUGHES, M., RIBBINS, P. and THOMAS, H. (1985) *Managing Education*. London: Holt, Rinehart and Winston.

MARLAND, M. (1986) *School Management Skills*. London: Heinemann Educational Books.

PAISEY, A. (1982) *School Organisation*, 2, 2, 180. London: Falmer Press.

3

Special Needs in the Classroom

Gary Thomas

'Support' has become the catchword for post-1981 Act thinking. Yet very little thought has been given to the way in which support should actually work in the classroom. If we consider all the problems which can arise when people share any task (in our case teaching) we should take seriously the possibility that support may come to be seen as one of those well-meant innovations which fell apart because nobody really examined how it would work in practice. After all, Geen (1985) has shown that team teaching atrophied because everyone was so busy considering the theoretical benefits of the system, that they neglected to look at the mechanisms which were needed to make it a success. And the theoretical benefits, and problems, of team teaching are akin to those of support teaching. The problems of teaming have been rehearsed elsewhere (for example, Thomas, 1985, 1986, 1987) and it is the intention in this chapter to try to help resolve some of those problems by considering the ways in which teaming might actually operate.

Before I go further I must make some simple restatements about 'special needs'. Only then can I go on to suggest how these needs might be better met with 'support'. Special needs are sometimes glibly talked about; indeed, 'SEN' has acquired the status of an adjective, with many of the same connotations as 'ESN'. There is a real need for some verbal hygiene if old attitudes are not to pervade the changes that are emerging. So, what are these 'special needs' in relation to the Warnock twenty per cent?

The answer can perhaps crudely be summarised as: *children who are experiencing difficulty with some aspect of the curriculum at school need extra teaching or different ways of teaching.* If we outline what some of these extra or different ways of teaching are, though, we immediately come up against problems. Let us list them and see:

Some children almost immediately forget what they have learned. They therefore need
- regular practice.

Also such children are often easily distracted and lose concentration very quickly. So they also need
- distributed practice, (for example eight five minute sessions are better than one forty minute session).

Many children seem to need
- absence from distraction; (this might be achieved through regrouping the children or through having a section of the room available for individualised teaching away from doors, windows etc.).

Children who are experiencing difficulty may also need
- more prompting, (i.e. providing as much help as necessary, making sure the task is successfully undertaken, so that errors are not rehearsed and the child finishes feeling good).

All children need
- a rewarding learning experience, but those who are having problems may need their teaching carefully examined in order to ensure that they are not repeatedly coming up against failure.

Problems in Organising the Integrated Classroom

It is immediately clear that these needs are going to be difficult to meet in a busy class of thirty or more children. As Galton and Simon (1980) say:

> It is simply not possible to structure and monitor the activities of thirty individual children simultaneously, in such a way as to ensure that the level of work of each is consistently appropriate (p.210).

If this was the case in the pre-1981 Act classroom, how much chance is there for the success of integration? The difficulty which so often arises when a child is integrated into the mainstream is captured in the teacher's heartfelt, 'What am I supposed to do with the other thirty?' Looking at most of these special needs, it is clear that what they boil down to is the need for more individual or small group help, and we therefore have defined our first problem: providing enough individual help. This problem, as we shall see, may be at least partly disentangled by considering how support teaching might work. But let us first try to define other problems.

It seems clear from research, such as that carried out in the ORACLE project (Galton, Simon and Croll, 1980), that teachers who are involved in a lot of individual work are, in general, less successful at managing the main body of the class than teachers who predominantly work as class teachers. Given that our first problem in meeting special needs was *providing enough individual help*, this is cause for immediate concern. We can perhaps then summarise our second problem: managing the rest of the class.

Management is all important. It is easy to say what individuals need; the problem is providing for those needs without having the rest of the class climbing up the walls. But the importance of management goes deeper than this: the interesting fact which emerges from research into teaching is that the teacher's personal organisation and management is crucial in overcoming – or at least in not generating – learning problems. Brophy and Evertson (1976) found that effective management skills were related not just to classroom behaviour but also to children's learning.

Changing conceptions of the teaching process now particularly emphasise the importance of management. Bennett (1987), for instance, in a wide-ranging review of the models which have been used to examine the teaching-learning process, concludes that much research has been of very limited utility. He goes on to say that current work is addressing issues to do with:

> the management of learning in terms of setting the scene and the organisation of resources, both material and human, to provide optimum learning environments (p.74).

Assimilating this idea should make those of us who work in special education both uncomfortable and optimistic. Uncomfortable, because an organisational orientation is alien for us: we have traditionally concentrated on analysing and remedying individual problems. We have not needed to focus on the organisational environment since the whole thrust of special education was in removing children from the natural environment and providing specialised help or therapy. It should however make us optimistic for two main reasons. First, there is precious little evidence that our traditional methods have been successful (see Thomas, 1985); and second, it is the organisational elements which at the present time hold out most promise of success (see DeVault *et al.*, 1977; Stallings *et al.*, 1986).

It is doubly important to consider organisation and management when considering the integrated classroom. Yet it is all too easy when reviewing educational research to propose what Smyth (1981) has called 'teacher-should statements'. But the dimensions of classroom management are now different. Perhaps what marks the difference between today's classrooms and those of ten years ago is a fundamentally changed dynamic – a dynamic invoked by the presence of additional adults. Often these additional people are present in the classroom in order to help meet special needs. Since organisation and management are so important it may be useful to pick out a few pieces of seminal research to demonstrate the strategies which effective teachers employ in successfully managing the class. Such a selection might serve as the basis for subsequent discussion on the organisation of the integrated classroom.

Both Kounin (1974) and Brophy (1979) stressed the importance of keeping the flow going in the classroom. Kounin particularly pointed to the competing demands on the teacher's attention, noting that good teachers manage these competing demands by being 'withit' and by overlapping (i.e. dealing with an interruption without breaking into the flow of the session). Brophy noted that successful teachers adopt a number of strategies to 'maximise time spent engaged in productive activities'. Among these are (i) the use of *grouping* and the placement of resources, and (ii) the use of techniques for *group monitoring* during individual instruction.

Anderson *et al.* (1980), like Kounin, found that withitness, maintenance of momentum and monitoring were all important. They also found that successful teachers quickly reviewed children's work by *regularly and systematically circulating* so that each child was checked frequently; also they systematically provided feedback. Less successful teachers were unsystematic in their circulation, mainly responding to those children who caught their attention. Weinstein (1979), in reviewing research on the physical environment of the school, points to the fact that most of the talking between teacher and children takes place at the centre and front of the classroom – even in open classrooms which in theory have no front. Here again is the need to circulate.

I shall draw on these findings in the following analysis.

Ways round the problems

We are now perhaps in a position to summarise some possible ways round the problems we have identified. To recall, the problems in integration (in all classrooms) are essentially about providing enough *individual help* of the right kind, at the same time as effectively *managing* the rest of the class. Let us list the ways of doing these things:

Individual help is best provided by:
  providing frequent short doses of help.

Managing the class is best done by:
  circulating frequently,
  providing frequent feedback to children on their work,
  providing alerting cues,
  intelligent use of grouping and placement of resources.

Support and Organisation

Since individual help and managing the body of the class are so difficult to provide simultaneously, there is clear opportunity for support teachers and staff from other support services to discuss with the teacher the possibility of each taking on one of these elements.

Perhaps even more importantly, there is scope here for useful discussion between the support teacher and the class teacher on ways of managing the class (and hence managing special needs, since as we noted above the two are inseparable) when the support teacher is not present. Support teachers will not be the only ones to become involved in this kind of discussion. Integration is about the specialist personnel, who have traditionally been helping children in the special sector, moving into the mainstream. This means that increasingly staff from all kinds of support services will be working alongside the class teacher to help meet special needs. At the same time, integration is bringing other people into the classroom: ancillary services of all kinds are now being appointed to help meet children's special needs. Integration is about teamwork.

Immediately, support teachers, and to a lesser extent personnel from support services , are placed in a difficult position. They are being asked not only to move from a withdrawal setting to a mainstream classroom setting, but they are being asked to negotiate with mainstream teachers – many of them quite content with the existing arrangements – on matters which have previously been the sole preserve of the mainstream teacher. Many class teachers might welcome the new arrangements and might be grateful for the insights and advice which this new cross-fertilisation brings, but others may react defensively, resenting the 'intrusion' of the support teacher. It is in these circumstances that the support teacher's reserves of tact and diplomacy will be in heaviest demand.

Tact and diplomacy are, however, on their own insufficient in moving to the new kinds of arrangements for meeting special needs. The new arrangements are, as I have discussed, about fundamentally changed classroom organisation and a very different way of conceptualising special needs. Tackling these new arrangements requires an analysis of the new situation within two separate sets of parameters. First, there are factors within the 'personal' situation, where negotiations about the new changes are going to take place. Second, there are 'substantial' matters; in other words, what the participants are going to be talking *about*.

Discussion and Negotiation

Essential for successful teamwork are the processes of planning, monitoring and evaluation (see for example Cohen, 1976). Without the participation of all team members – and not just the professionals – in these processes there is unlikely to be meaningful involvement. In practice it will be difficult for teachers to find time for planning and evaluation with others. But the warnings are clear: if time is not found, this kind of complex collaborative exercise is likely to end in failure. It may well be that support teachers in particular (as those who will find it most difficult to find time for this kind of exercise) will have to earmark time for planning and monitoring in the re-scheduling of their work.

These developments are so new in education that there are few examples from which to draw in seeking advice on the best ways of going about these processes of negotiation. But there is advice to be gleaned from the ways in which groups work in other settings (for example, Hackman and Oldham, 1980; Robson, 1982; Herkimer, 1984). Key elements appear to be in communication, in acceptance of the ideas of others, and a willingness to make changes. These may seem so obvious as elements of successful teamwork that it is hardly worth mentioning them, but it is all too clear that unless they are explicitly spelt out they are often ignored: the obvious eludes us and commonsense flies out of the window when we work under the weight of the organisational culture. These 'obvious' elements might be incorporated into the new teamworking arrangements thus (from Thomas, 1988):

1 The team (comprising perhaps a class teacher, a support teacher and a parent) meet to discuss the way they are going to work. Others, such as the headteacher or the educational psychologist, might also be involved. Some kind of structure is essential for this meeting if it is not to become a mini case conference postulating quasi-diagnostic explanations for individual children's problems. The focus is most usefully organisational. People need to discuss the roles they are to be fulfilling and whether, for instance, they would feel comfortable undertaking a particular set of tasks. Depending on the composition of the group, curricular issues might be discussed – for instance, how the support teacher is going to make adaptations to the mainstream curriculum for children with reading difficulties.

2 The planned scheme is put into operation. Participants are encouraged to be looking for problems and ways of improving the new way of working. People should be encouraged to remember that the system is not sacrosanct; it has merely been devised as a way of effectively meeting special needs. As such it has to be adapted as problems are seen to arise.

3 The team meets again to discuss the running of the system. The openness of a 'quality circle' should be a hallmark of such a meeting; in other words, the atmosphere should be informal with people being encouraged to come up with ideas. Such a meeting ought to take place regularly – at first perhaps once a week.

The 'Substantial' Matters

Given that there are not too many problems in this process of discussion and planning, what will be the substance of the discussions that take place? The new perspective on special needs demands that we seek to identify needs – not children

– and that we seek to forge solutions to those needs out of changes in classroom organisation.

One of the most fruitful starting points in this process is in considering the physical arrangement of the class. In looking at place and learning I can use part of a short study which I have made in a primary classroom (see Thomas, 1985). In this classroom I looked at how much children were on-task (i.e. doing what they were supposed to be doing). The results in terms of place and learning are summarised in Figure 3.1.

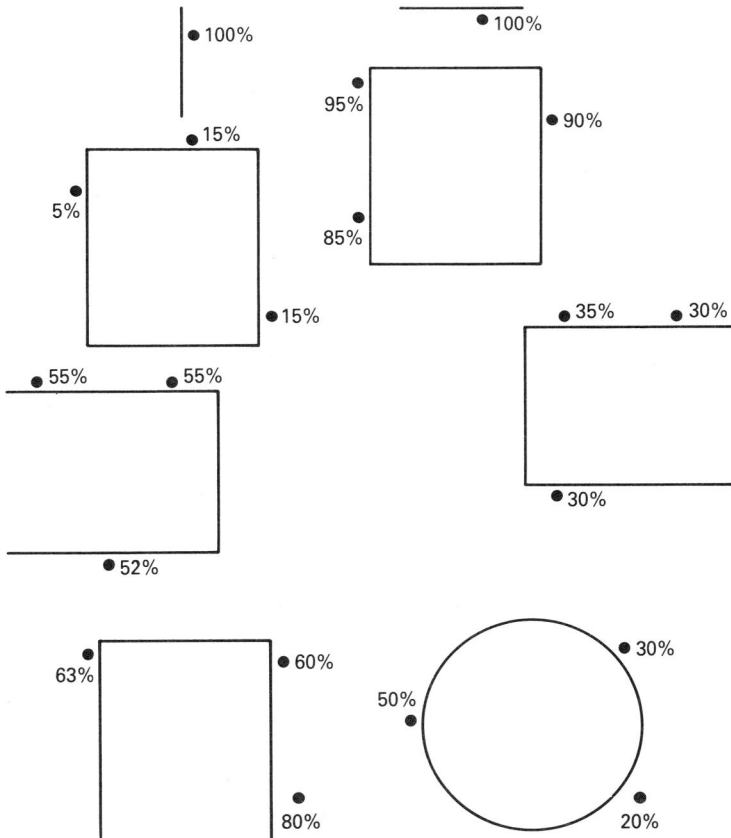

Figure 3.1 Amount of time children were 'on-task' in a primary classroom.

Two interesting points emerge from this analysis: the first is that those children who are sitting on their own or at the periphery of the classroom activity are, in general, more on-task than those who are in groups; the second point is that those who are in groups have roughly similar on-task levels. The reason for this latter point became evident when I examined the videotapes on which these figures are based – groups were facilitating in many cases the kind of activity which, as teachers, we try to minimise; activities which children usually characterise as 'messing around'.

This leads to the question *why group?*. The answer of course lies in the principles which have for many years guided the good Plowden classroom. We want to foster communication, cooperation and imagination, usually through groupwork. But research (see for example Tann, 1988) backs up what any experienced observer of the primary classroom knows: children are often being asked to do *individual work* in groups. If this is the case there is little or no point in grouping. Children concentrate on individual work better on an individual basis.

Groups are ubiquitous in the British primary school. But integration is perhaps providing the stimulus for re-examining the reasons for such grouping. Indeed it seems that much of this re-examination is coincidentally occurring at a time when many are re-examining, for different reasons, the foundations upon which certain Plowden recommendations were made (see Bennett, 1978). These considerations have immediate implications for classroom organisation. There is scope for thinking about the deployment of space within the classroom and the best arrangements of that space for helping children who are experiencing difficulties. For instance, instead of putting display tables and cupboards 'horizontally' against the wall, they might be moved out so that they serve the dual function of providing screens and partitions. Easily distracted children – the 'intermittent workers' of the ORACLE study – may work better if distractions are reduced by this kind of manoeuvre.

The classroom geography is also important in terms of the need for circulation by the teacher (an important characteristic of good teaching). It is important not to stay static but rather to circulate amongst the children, while at the same time being able to keep an eye on all. The cubby holes and partitions we have just created, then, must not be *too* private. Linked with the classroom geography are the tasks we expect children to

do. It has been realised since the work of Johnson *et al.*
(1983) that merely putting children into integrated settings and
expecting them to get on with it is not enough. Indeed, merely
moving special children to ordinary classrooms may have very
different effects from those we expect. Johnson *et al.* show that
handicapped pupils are viewed in negative ways whether they
are in mainstream classes or not. Physical proximity carries with
it the possibility of making things worse rather than better. The
success of integration schemes seems to depend a great deal on
how instruction is organised and how interaction is structured.

There is a need, then, to consider how children may best be
placed within the reorganised classroom. It is outside the scope
of this chapter to go into the ways in which this might be done
but the reader is referred to Aaronson and Bridgeman (1979) and
Tann (1988) for a fuller discussion of this issue. Suffice it to say
that the most important need is for a consideration of the aims
of a particular session for a child or a group of children, and
a matching of task and setting. In other words, if children –
with or without special needs – are being expected to work
individually, then they are best placed in settings where they
can work with little distraction. If the expectation is for a group
activity, the task should be organised so that all the children
are able to participate meaningfully. The classroom organisation
may be built around the expectations for the session.

There is another important reason for considering place
when teaching within the classroom: the removal of stigma
and the promotion of integration. Returning for a moment
to the point made earlier in this chapter, special needs, as
it would have been seen in the traditional sense, implied the
identification of a specific set of children. Now it implies more
an identification of need rather than an identification of children.
The implication is that specific groups or sets of children are
not identified within special needs 'ghettos' in the classroom.
Rather, it is assumed that because special needs may arise with
one child at one time and with another child at another time,
'problems' will not be collected in a particular area. Special
needs will be tackled as and when they arise.

Orchestrating the Efforts of Others

Let us return now to a point made at the beginning of this
chapter. I mentioned the difficulty of providing for special

needs at the same time as managing the main body of the class and that the new teaming arrangements emerging give rise to the possibility of people taking on specialised roles within the classroom. Through this specialisation, the problems which have hitherto arisen when individual help is required are minimised. What form might the specialisation take? Looking both at the learning needs outlined earlier and at the literature on classroom management, a rationale for two distinct roles may be drawn up.

The first role is for someone working with individual children. Given the need for regular and distributed work, this person will be working with individual children for short periods of time – perhaps five to fifteen minutes – taking the children on a rota and having prepared materials to work from. The second role is for someone concentrating on the engagement of the class as a whole. Since the principal difficulty in managing a class seems to be in providing individual help at the same time, there are clear implications for the way that this person operates. Clearly there will be no purpose in having established any differentiation in the work of the adult participants unless cognisance is taken of this fact. In order to prevent the same kinds of problems emerging, this person's 'job specification' will exclude any in-depth work with individuals. Rather, it will take in the features of good classroom management outlined earlier: it will specify that the person should circulate quickly, providing feedback to children both on work and behaviour as frequently as possible.

Immediately, there are curricular implications in this kind of specialised work. Those children who are the responsibility of the 'group manager' cannot be undertaking tasks which require a great deal of help. Rather, they will need to be consolidating ideas which have been taught in other situations, or doing less formal work which requires less direct input from an adult. A host of caveats and qualifications need to be introduced in discussing the work of different classroom participants in this way. It is dangerous to be at all prescriptive, given the differences which occur in classroom situations. Each classroom is unique, with a unique set of children, problems and staff, and it is meaningless to suggest that something which will work in one situation will necessarily work in another. However, if the new teaming arrangements are to have any chance of succeeding, it is essential that the parameters of classroom organisation are discussed among the various participants. If they are not, the ambiguities and uncertainties which seem to have been at least in part responsible for the demise of team teaching will surface to smother our best endeavours to implement integration.

Conclusions

Special education has taken a new direction in its espousal of the ideal of integration. The new direction demands a complete reappraisal of the way in which we have looked at children's problems. In many ways the new perspective is simpler – more pragmatic. There is less pseudo-scientific jargon about learning disabilities; there is no longer resort to psychological and medical notions in 'explaining' children's difficulties in learning. Although the new focus is simpler, specifying children's learning needs in commonsense language, it confronts those of us working in special needs with new challenges. We are increasingly going to have to seek solutions to problems in the natural environment of the mainstream classroom, with all its existing difficulties. We are going to have to seek solutions in the new teamwork that is emerging. This chapter can only have been a pointer to the kinds of factors which may form the focus of the new analysis. Ultimately solutions will be found in specific arrangements and in particular circumstances where teachers and others devise individual strategies for managing their own unique set of problems.

References

AARONSON, E. and BRIDGEMAN, D. (1979) 'Jigsaw groups and the desegregated classroom: in pursuit of common goals', *Personality and Social Psychology Bulletin*, 5, 4, 438-46.

ANDERSON, L.M., EVERTSON, C.M. and EMMER, E.T. (1980) 'Dimensions in classroom management derived from recent research', *Journal of Curriculum Studies*, 12, 4, 343-56.

BENNETT, S.N. (1978) 'Recent research on teaching: a dream, a belief, a model', *British Journal of Educational Psychology*, 48, 127-47.

BROPHY, J. (1979) 'Advances in teacher research', *Journal of Classroom Interaction*, 15, 1, 1-7.

COHEN, E.G. (1976) 'Problems and prospects of teaming', *Educational Research Quarterly*, 1, 2, 49-63.

DeVAULT, M.L., HARNISCHFEGER, A. and WILEY, D.E. (1977) *Curricula, Personnel Resources and Grouping Strategies*. St Ann, Mo.: ML-Group for Policy Studies in Education, Central Midwestern Regional Lab.

GALTON, M.J. and SIMON, B. (1980) *Progress and Performance in the Primary Classroom*. London: Routledge and Kegan Paul.

GALTON, M.J., SIMON, B. and CROLL, P. (1980) *Inside the Primary Classroom*. London: Routledge and Kegan Paul.

GEEN, A.G. (1985) 'Team teaching in the secondary schools of England and Wales', *Educational Review*, 37, 1, 29-38.

HACKMAN, J.R. and OLDHAM, G.R. (1980) *Work Redesign*. Reading, Ma.: Addison-Wesley.

HERKIMER, A.G. 1984) 'Quality circles in healthcare provision,' *Healthcare Financial Management*, 38, 7, 34-39.

JOHNSON, D.W., JOHNSON, R.T. and MARUYAMA, G. (1983) 'Independence and interpersonal attraction among heterogeneous and homogeneous individuals: a theoretical formulation and a meta-analysis of the research', *Review of Educational Research*, 53, 1, 5-54.

KOUNIN, K.S. and GUMP, P.V. (1974) 'Signal systems of lesson settings and the task related behaviour of pre-school children', *Journal of Educational Psychology*, 66, 4, 554-62.

ROBSON, M. (1982) *Quality Circles: A Practical Guide*. Aldershot: Gower.

SMYTH, W.J. (1981) 'Research on classroom management: studies of pupil engaged learning time as a special but instructive case', *Journal of Education for Teaching*, 7, 2, 127-48.

STALLINGS, J., ROBBINS, P., PRESBREY, L. and SCOTT, J. (1986) 'Effects of instruction based on the Madeline Hunter model on students' achievement: findings from a follow-through project', *Elementary School Journal*, 86, 5, 571-87.

TANN, S. (1988) 'Grouping and the integrated classroom' in THOMAS, G. and FEILER, A. *Planning for Special Needs*. Oxford: Basil Blackwell.

THOMAS, G. (1985) 'Room management in mainstream education', *Educational Research*, 27, 3, 186-94.

THOMAS, G. (1986) 'Integrating personnel in order to integrate children', *Support for Learning*, 1, 1, 19-27.

THOMAS, G. (1988) 'Extra people in the primary classroom', *Educational Research*, 29, 3, 173-82.

WEINSTEIN, C.S. (1979) 'The physical environment of the school: a review of the research', *Review of Educational Research*, 49, 4, 577-610.

4

Special Needs in Reading

Olive Robinson

No teacher will deny the importance of reading as a fundamental requirement for learning in school. All teachers recognise the sad fact that children with reading difficulties can be left lagging behind their peers and possibly failing dismally in their academic work. Even more sad is the fact that these children increasingly think of themselves as failures as they progress through school and this affects their motivation and sometimes their behaviour, causing a greater complication of problems.

The special help that is traditionally provided for such children at primary level is usually very different from that offered at secondary level, and often neither can be called adequate. In the primary school, the class teacher too often has to cope with large classes and does not have the time to deal consistently with special individual difficulties. Where special help is provided, it is often on a peripatetic basis which can reduce special individual or group provision to as little as half-an-hour a week. At secondary level where the supply of specialist teachers and resources, though far from adequate, has commonly been more generous, the presence of a special needs department has frequently led to a situation where the reading problems of children have become the total responsibility of specialist teachers and scant regard has been given to those problems in the mainstream classroom.

However, since the 1981 Education Act began to be implemented in 1983, there have been the slow beginnings of change. In some areas a great deal of thought and planning has gone into better provision of materials for the less able reader and special needs teachers have left the isolation of the special help unit (under whatever name) and are beginning to take their place alongside mainstream teachers in the ordinary classroom, helping, advising and supporting both teacher and children. In other areas special needs teachers have been appointed and a system of partial withdrawal for special help has been implemented for the first time. In many places there are now special teaching teams who, under a variety of names, visit primary schools to advise and support. However, all is not yet well and children with reading difficulties continue to exist and to fail at all levels of the education system.

It is not possible to explain adequately the reasons for such failure: it could be said that there are as many reasons as there are failures. Nevertheless it is true to say that each one is capable of improvement and it is possible to adopt methods that will help raise the reading levels of most children. To do this, it is important to remember that children with reading difficulties have to suffer their difficulties nearly all the time in school and thus continually require particular consideration for their problems, regardless of the subject being taught and whether the teacher is a reading specialist or not.

Research into the reading processes carried out over the last two decades by people like Frank Smith (1971, 1973) and Lunzer and Gardner (1979) has given rise to much practical help and advice. From this teachers have learned that the majority of children learn to read by the practical process of reading themselves and through the use of language. It is essential that reading materials should match the reading needs of individual children and that the language used should always be relevant and opportunities created to familiarise pupils with the language that is used. Emphasis should be on success with a minimum of negative comment and a maximum input of positive encouragement. It can be seen therefore that there is a responsibility for the teacher to know the reading requirements of the children in the class and to supply appropriate materials. It is also necessary to monitor progress so that the levels of materials and pupils are always matched and keep pace with each other. In order to encourage motivation, a sense of achievement, and the necessary building up of self-esteem and confidence, children must 'become the masters of words and not allow words to become their masters'. To achieve this, there must be relevance and interest, good language development and access to materials that are well-presented and appropriate. How can this be encouraged by the classroom teacher?

It is useful to look at developments that are gradually taking place in the classroom. The 1981 Act followed the Warnock Report (DES, 1978) and took from it the recommendation for the integration of children with special educational needs into the ordinary (mainstream) school. This worried a great number of teachers. It was envisaged that ill-resourced and ill-equipped teachers would have to cope with an ever growing number of children with disabilities, both physical and intellectual. Many teachers felt that they had not been trained to deal with the problems that such integration would incur. What is now beginning to be recognised is the fact that many of the children defined as being in special educational need under the Warnock recommendations are, and always have been, attending ordinary schools. But this does not necessarily mean that these children have been appropriately educated, and it is just as important to reconsider their needs as it is to assess the needs of any 'integrated' pupil. Generally speaking, teachers are quite right to say that they do not have appropriate resources for the children, that money is scarce, and that staff are poorly trained to assess the pupils and apply relevant teaching methods. However, it remains that if the children are present in the classroom, then it is the responsibility of the teacher to teach them and, as has been noted, an ability to read effectively is necessary if learning is to take place in school. It would be helpful, therefore, to look at three areas:

1 Appropriate assessment of children with reading difficulties who need special help.
2 An appraisal of organisation in the school and in the classroom to ensure the promotion of good learning behaviour for *all* pupils.
3 The adoption of relevant methods and materials to match the needs of children.

Assessment

The most common form of assessing the reading ability of children is through the use of tests, either individually or in a group. While some forms of testing can be of value, their use can also be damaging for the pupil if it results in labelling and categorising. Teachers often feel quite apprehensive about having children with reading problems in their classes because they feel unable to teach reading. This is understandable when reading is commonly viewed as being a series of sub-skills in which the children are tested for competence and are then given practice in those sub-skills where they have been shown to be deficient.

This 'deficit model' teaching thus confronts children with areas in which they have persistently failed and makes a mystique of the teaching of reading for non-specialist staff. It means that a pupil with reading difficulties has to wait for a time when a particular teacher is available, while at all other times the real reading experience from printed materials can be neglected. Reading thus becomes a separate, mechanical lesson. It cannot be emphasised too strongly that these children live with their difficulties the whole time and not only need, but deserve help in all aspects of the curriculum if any degree of real success is to be achieved. Michael Marland (Lunzer and Gardner, 1979) notes that:

> . . . only a whole school policy can hope to succeed significantly. The teaching of speaking, reading and writing is . . . an important part of every teacher's responsibility . . . It is the job of every teacher to ensure that a pupil understands what he teaches, and therefore if he uses any print material, it is his responsibility to make sure that it is understood from the text (i.e. not merely by the teacher short-circuiting the text by alternative verbal explanation) (p.277).

And in the Bullock Report (DES, 1975) it is clearly stated that:

> Remedial help in learning to read should, wherever possible, be closely related to the rest of the child's learning.

The special needs teacher has an important function as an advisor, enabling the mainstream teacher to understand that the teaching of reading does not consist of testing and teaching sub-skills, but upon a variety of other factors to which the classroom teacher can make a valuable contribution. This will require a close assessment of classroom organisation, teaching situations and the supply of appropriate printed materials as well as the development of an ability to assess progress. Thomson (Stott, 1978) in summarising the Stott hypothesis writes:

> Learning failures may well be a product of inappropriate behaviours in the learning situation . . . and what we should be doing . . . is looking not at test scores, but at the child's problem-solving behaviour . . . to monitor progress and note crucial points of improvement (p.116).

Learning failure may well be related to difficulties with reading. Children with reading problems often lack the ability to organise materials, to sequence their work on paper and to understand fully what is required of them from printed instructions. Therefore to assess effectively the reading behaviour of children in the classroom, it is necessary to observe how they cope with printed materials and make use of them. This, in turn, requires the development of an efficient form of monitoring so that interest, achievement and progress may be recorded and used as a basis for the further supply of material and method. Monitoring, if effectively maintained, can also indicate when and where additional teaching is needed.

Organisation

To develop this kind of approach a re-assessment of classroom organisation, and perhaps teaching method, has to be considered if reading across the curriculum is to improve and become more effective. The presence of children with reading difficulties in a class often means that their needs are neglected while the teacher attends to the needs of the rest of the class, or that their needs become paramount and take priority over the rest of the class. However, this need not be so. The presence of such children can provide the teacher with an incentive to think about improving the reading performance of the class as a whole. This is what Warnock calls functional integration:

> Functional integration makes the greatest demands upon a school, since it requires the most careful planning of class and individual teaching programmes to ensure that *all* children might benefit, whether or not they have special educational needs (DES, 1978).

The establishment of a whole class approach requires the most careful and rigorous planning since it involves consideration of the needs of individuals and provision for them within the context of class and group activity. Its framework needs first to be discussed and adopted by the whole school so that all children and every teacher might benefit from a clearly defined common aim and a structured network of support. Organisation within the classroom can then be contemplated and adapted to make optimum use of supporting adults, team teaching, paired teaching or, when a teacher is working alone, to enable that teacher to use appropriate materials and methods. Many of these aspects are dealt with elsewhere in this book, but for the purposes of this chapter it might be useful to consider how teachers throughout a school could be kept in touch with information and advice about the diagnosed learning needs of children who have problems. This kind of organisation is perhaps particularly important where the special needs teaching team is too small to cater adequately for the large number of differing needs that are always arising throughout the school. Such a situation can result in class teachers being left to manage on their own, feeling uneasy and lonely, and very often promotes a feeling of boredom in the pupils who are 'contained' rather than taught. The organisation required is one that will assess problems and set up a monitoring structure: a key factor in the structure would seem to be a form of communication that is both efficient and practical. For this, a well-organised special needs team is required whose role and function is agreed and understood by the school as a whole. Historically, the special needs or 'remedial' teacher has been

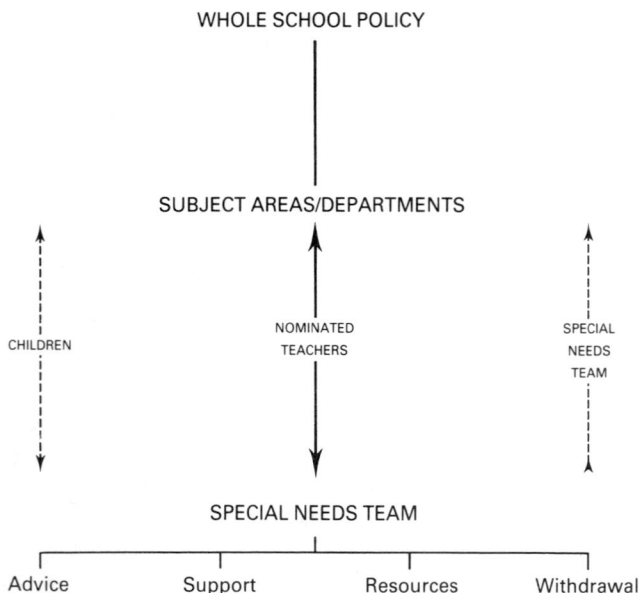

WHOLE SCHOOL POLICY

SUBJECT AREAS/DEPARTMENTS

CHILDREN

NOMINATED
TEACHERS

SPECIAL
NEEDS
TEAM

SPECIAL NEEDS TEAM

Advice   Support   Resources   Withdrawal

Figure 4.1   This model demonstrates how a whole school approach can involve all subject areas in the monitoring of children with special needs and cater for them across the curriculum

given low status within the staff structure of the secondary school (Sewell, 1982). The proposed structure would effectively remove the team from the comparative isolation of their department and make them more accountable to the school as a whole: their expertise would be seen and their value possibly re-assessed.

Figure 4.1 illustrates a possible structure. It can be seen that each department nominates a teacher who will liaise with the special needs team. Any member of staff within a department may consult the nominated teacher about any pupil who appears to be experiencing a difficulty with a particular subject to an extent where special help may be required. As a result, the nominated teacher may decide to refer the pupil to the special needs team and will give them all relevant information and samples of the pupil's work, together with an outline of the content of the lesson or lessons in which the difficulties are most apparent. The special needs team will then see the pupil and try to assess the nature and extent of the problem and after discussion with the referring department, will decide upon one or more of the following strategies:

1 To support the pupil in the subject by sending a teacher/helper to work with him/her in specific lessons.
2 To support the class teacher by arranging for a special needs teacher to attend specified lessons on a teacher-partnership basis, working with the whole class.
3 To produce and adapt materials for the subject so that the pupil can use them with greater confidence.
4 To help and advise the subject teacher about materials, methods and practices that would be appropriate for the difficulties being experienced.
5 To withdraw the pupil for special help on the subject for a specified length of time.
6 To make a survey of the materials used in the subject area and to enable the department to match the materials to the needs of individual pupils.

It can be seen that this system would also enable support staff to appreciate the problems of the class teacher which could result in help that would not only benefit the special needs of individual children, but might also be of practical use to the class as a whole. Clearly, within the system or any that is devised, it is important to implement and maintain a record of the response and progress of all referred children, so that each one is monitored, and advice and all forms of support are seen to be working effectively. If the children do not show signs of progress over a period of time, then a re-appraisal of their situation becomes necessary.

Methods and Materials

Once a support and monitoring structure has been organised, attention can be focused upon ways of using and developing reading skills in the mainstream classroom. Transition from the development of a policy and its planning to its practical implementation is not easy and can be beset by problems. Some of these can, however, be anticipated and catered for so that their effect can perhaps be minimised. Possibly the greatest problem can be that of staff commitment, and it is at the point of transfer to the classroom of a whole school approach to the development of reading that the importance of staff commitment is realised. Research has suggested that low-expectation pupils receive less encouragement and more criticism from their teachers than high-expectation pupils. Teachers themselves have minimum expectations of such pupils and unwittingly communicate this to them, thus creating a relationship that expects and accepts a mediocre performance (Brophy and Good, 1974).

It is necessary to gain the support of the majority of staff in any proposed change and often a programme of in-service education is required to enable staff to understand the reasons for change and the benefits it might bring to both staff and pupils. Fortunately, in primary schools and within most departments at secondary level, there are teachers who are sympathetic to children with learning problems and it is to these teachers that a school can turn when first promoting the practice of a whole school approach (Sewell, 1982). The personalities of skilled and sympathetic teachers are of value in forwarding the progress of the less able and they can achieve a great deal. At the same time it is necessary for them to maintain a regular dialogue with the special needs staff, not only for the purposes discussed elsewhere in this chapter, but because an exchange of information and ideas can help to sustain motivation and confidence in a classroom teacher who, understandably, may be feeling cautious about tackling learning difficulties.

One of the important difficulties that a less able reader

often experiences is an inability to perceive the relationship between the spoken and the printed word. Constructive and regular practice in the use of language is a valuable asset in the acquisition of fluent reading. It is important therefore to regard reading as an extension of language (Smith, 1971). Experience with adult literacy classes demonstrates that talk and discussion can be a useful starting point both for the reader and the teacher. Pupils always bring with them language and experience which can provide and sustain motivation if purposefully directed. From this, it is clear that some language activity and discussion is necessary if effective reading is to be achieved.

Such discussion is difficult to manage unless it is carried out in small groups. Within each group there can be a range of resources and the composition of the groups need not remain static in any series of lessons. Each group can be provided with appropriate stimuli, such as a tape-recording, an object or piece of apparatus, a cartoon strip etc., which should support relevant textual material. The teacher should introduce the topic for discussion and there should be clear instructions regarding the purpose of the group discussion or language-based activity. This can be free-flowing around a particular theme, or more precisely defined for a purpose or an end product which is clearly understood by the whole class.

It would be of value here to consider the nature of materials that can be supplied for small group work in addition to those already mentioned. Although it has been made clear in this chapter that materials need to match the reading requirements of individual pupils in the classroom, it is nonetheless interesting to note the response of those same individuals to texts of different content and interest which may be of a higher reading level, for example, the sports pages of some newspapers or magazines about pop and rock music. Within a small group it has been suggested that printed matter need not correspond with the level of the least able reader and indeed such organisation can have the advantage of introducing a wide variety of broadly based texts. Thus, source material can be taken from journals, magazines, newspapers etc., as well as text books, provided it is relevant and well-presented. However, experience has found that the composition of small groups requires sensitive planning. The needs of some pupils whose personalities, reading rates, and developing abilities to detect inferential meaning from reading material, must also be considered. These pupils may perhaps be given texts of greater complexity, or at times be given individual work to do on a tutorial basis – this is particularly true for older secondary pupils.

Within a small group approach, however, most children of whatever ability can make surprising progress when they experience a collaborative and participatory way into relevant texts. When discussion about text, stimuli and purpose takes place between pupils, and is generated by them, they become actively involved with the reading process and are no longer passive receivers of information, as they often are when listening or reading as individuals. The activity gives pupils time to pause and reflect upon the text – which is one of the most important aspects of effective reading – and then to make informed and intelligent guesses which are measured and tested against it (Lunzer and Gardner, 1979). It provides an active reading method which is more effective because it involves the readers, as a group, in a search for meaning. An interesting teaching approach for small group work, Directed Activities Related to Texts (DARTS) outlines a structure and method of group teaching which has been used successfully with groups in science, English, humanities and in the special needs area (Davies and Greene, 1982, 1984). This approach, involving cloze procedure, sequencing and prediction was introduced to the United Kingdom by Christopher Walker, whose book *Reading Development and Extension* (1974) remains essential reading for interested teachers. In considering the approach, it is worth while reminding ourselves that in our classrooms we have a number of children who apparently can read, but consistently fail to grasp adequately the meaning of their reading. They concentrate on getting the words right. This has become known as 'barking at print', where the emphasis is on the correct decoding of the printed word rather than on the meaning of the context in which the word is used. Some traditional methods of teaching reading, which insist that a child pauses at an unfamiliar word and concentrates on 'building it up', can actually hinder the process of 'reading for meaning'. It is important to realise that children have an ability from a very early age to use sentences that are grammatically correct (Feiler and Thomas, 1980). This ability helps them to use contextual cues and if given the opportunity to guess an unfamiliar word in context, most children will suggest one which, even if it is not the one on the page, is one that will provide appropriate meaning to the text. The teacher of any subject, at any level, should use this knowledge to help the child with reading difficulties, and the more fluent reader to develop further reading strategies.

Small group work should actively involve each group member. In some activities it may be necessary for the teacher, in consultation with the group, to nominate members to take on certain responsibilities within it, particularly if texts contain detailed instructions for the work that is to be carried out, for example, interviewer, note-taker, recorder, collectors of data etc. Other group activities can be focused more directly on the text but still provide stimulus for discussion in order to arrive at a particular outcome. The use of 'cloze' passages and sequencing exercises are especially appropriate here. While group activities are in progress, the teacher can take the opportunity to observe closely the ways in which the children respond to the situation and the tasks that are set. This can provide much insight into the ways in which individuals organise materials, conceptualise and hypothesise, and their 'problem-solving' behaviour can be more fully understood. It can also show up hitherto unrealised reading problems (Lunzer and Gardner, 1979) and is an excellent time to carry out monitoring procedures on reading behaviour.

As work within the groups should be purposeful, so should the outcomes, if motivation is to be sustained. Groups can contribute to whole class projects, create their own group projects, produce papers/magazines of varying kinds, give informed views, suggest appropriate follow-up activities, use material for debates, use the group to help clarify understanding for revision purposes, and produce further individual work at a later time, etc. Whatever the outcomes are, all groups should realise that each group member is accountable to his/her own group and that there is a report-back system to their teacher(s) and to their peers for each group as a whole. This 'report-back' system must be unavoidable and can be included towards the end of the lesson, or as a separate follow-up lesson. It is clear, therefore, that the planning of outcomes and methods of reporting-back needs to be included in the preparation work of the teacher for group activity lessons. A useful method for conducting group work can be found in Barnes (1976), and Johnson and Johnson (1982).

Parental Involvement

The involvement of parents in the education of their children has recently acquired a new significance and importance, but their involvement at the level where learning takes place is not a new idea. Over the past decade much work has been done which points to the fact that parents can help to improve the reading abilities of their children considerably, through the initiation of paired and shared reading schemes (cf. Morgan and Lyon, 1979; Tizard, Schofield and Hewison, 1982). The adoption of appropriate ways of involving parents is described in the chapter on talking and writing, but here it is necessary to say that parents can be involved successfully at secondary as well as at primary level and that the benefits are many. Children can make good progress with their reading and also gain in confidence and self-esteem, and parents can become motivated and more understanding of the child's problems and of the teaching situation.

Conclusion

Finally, it is clear that children with reading difficulties present those difficulties to *all* who teach them. The nature of the problems may be mild or moderately severe, but whatever they are, it is the responsibility of all teachers to tackle them. The development of a whole school policy goes a long way towards the recognition of this fact and out of it may come a clear-headed, positive approach that will help to improve the reading abilities of all our children.

References

BARNES, D. (1976) *From Communication to Curriculum.* Harmondsworth: Penguin Books.

BROPHY, J.E. and GOOD, T.L. (1974) *Teacher Student Relationships: Causes and Consequences.* New York: Holt, Rinehart and Winston.

DAVIES, F. and GREENE, T. (1982) 'Effective reading: using pupil resources for comprehension and learning', *Remedial Education, 17*, 4, 163-70.

DAVIES, F. and GREENE, T. (1984) *Reading for Learning in the Sciences*, Schools Council. Edinburgh: Oliver and Boyd.

DEPARTMENT OF EDUCATION AND SCIENCE (1975) *A Language for Life* (Bullock Report). London: HMSO.

DEPARTMENT OF EDUCATION AND SCIENCE (1978) *Special Educational Needs* (Warnock Report). London: HMSO.

FEILER, A. and THOMAS, G. (1980) 'Teaching children to read – time to de-specialise', *Remedial Education, 15*, 2, 61-5.

JOHNSON, F.P. and JOHNSON, D.W. (1982) *Joining Together: Group Theory and Group Skills* (2nd edition). London: Prentice Hall.

LUNZER, E.A. and GARDNER, K. (1979) *The Effective Use of Reading.* London: Heinemann.

MARLAND, M. (1979) extract from 'Statement of policy' in LUNZER, E. and GARDNER, K. *The Effective Use of Reading.* London: Heinemann.

MORGAN, R. and LYON, E. (1979) 'Paired reading', *Child Psychology*, 5, 181-97.

SEWELL, G. (1982) *Reshaping Remedial Education.* Beckenham: Croom Helm.

SMITH, F. (1971) *Understanding Reading.* New York: Holt, Rinehart and Winston.

STOTT, D. (1978) *Helping Children with Learning Difficulties.* London: Ward Lock Educational.

TIZARD, J., SCHOFIELD, W.N. and HEWISON, J. (1982) 'Collaboration between teachers and parents in assisting children's reading', *British Journal of Educational Psychology*, 52, 1-15.

WALKER, C. (1974) *Reading Development and Extension.* London: Ward Lock Educational.

5
Special Needs in Talking and Writing
Katy Simmons

Children with learning difficulties can often be reluctant writers. They will join in enthusiastically with class discussions, only to complain loudly when the time comes to do some writing. 'Why do we have to *write* about this? Why can't we just go on *talking*?' Alternatively, they will be impatient with the teacher's attempts to get a discussion going. How many animated classroom talking sessions have come to an abrupt halt when a voice from the back says, 'Will we have to write about this?' Children often suspect, with some justification, that talk is simply a means to another end. What teachers *really* want them to do is write. If that is the aim, why then don't we all stop wasting time and go directly to the real task?

Children with learning difficulties often see little link between the spoken and the written word. They see no purpose in writing, other than to meet the demands of their teacher. This chapter looks at the ways in which the teacher may set about establishing links between what children say and what they write down. In establishing these links, the teacher will establish purposes for writing, which in turn will create the motivation that children with learning difficulties often need so badly.

Children's Knowledge of Language

Underlying this chapter is a conviction that children, when they come to school, already know a great deal about language, though they are unlikely to be able to describe this knowledge formally. Textbooks on child language would call their grasp of syntax and tense *metalinguistic awareness* rather than grammatical knowledge. A simple experiment in the classroom will show that children, even of limited ability, have quite extensive knowledge of the way their language works.

Using a set of pictures as a stimulus, ask a group of children to tell a story onto a tape-recorder. The individual stories should then be transcribed *verbatim*, complete with grammatical inaccuracies, inconsistencies and hesitations. At the next session, the transcribed stories should be handed back to the children and the question posed, 'Does this look like the sort of language you would find in a book?' The children will immediately recognise the features of spoken language that are out of place in a written story. Their comments will vary depending on age and ability, but they are almost certain to reflect a good grasp of what might be called 'grammatical' knowledge of an implicit kind. When this exercise was tried out on two twelve-year-olds, Wayne and Matthew, these were the stories they told onto the tape-recorder:

One day the village yobbos went down to the village to the telephone box and dared each other to phone the fire brigade. When the fireman came they looked around wondering what was wrong. He saw one of the children. Two of the yobbos legged it down the street. The firemen were very angry and they wondered who was to blame. They caught two of the children and asked who did it. They started to argue so they took them to their parents. (Matthew)

There's these three ... er ... four ... children called Tom, Wayne, Roger and Lucy and they all phoned up the firebrigade as a laugh in the telephone box and when the firebrigade came they hid everywhere where they could find, not too far away so they could see what happens and their reactions but they got caught as two were trying to run away the other two got caught. The passer-by saw the fire brigade catching them and then heard them say 'It's her' and things and the passer-by said 'I know where they live' and took them to their parents and they got sent to bed. (Wayne)

Subsequent discussion raised many useful points and showed that the children had a clear awareness of the difference between spoken and written language. Their discussion included:

– The need for appropriate vocabulary. Were 'yobbos' and 'legging it' suitable words for use in a written passage?
– Awareness of ambiguity. Who were all the 'theys' mentioned in Wayne's passage? In spoken language, the subject can be

indicated by gesture. In written passages, it is the grammar of the sentence which clears up ambiguity.

- Awareness of tense. The children soon spotted the inconsistencies of tense in Wayne's story.
- Use of the definite and indefinite article. In Wayne's story, the passer-by had not been mentioned before. The children were aware that they should therefore write 'a' passer-by.

These, and a number of other points, made for a useful, interesting discussion. Both Wayne and Matthew had learning difficulties and were receiving extra help. Yet their insight into grammatical correctness was considerable and the whole exercise demonstrated that children are, in fact, sophisticated language users.

Teaching as a data-gathering activity

Analysis of children's work can provide the teacher with considerable insight into the language processes that children are using. Rather than starting off with ideas of 'correctness' where children with learning difficulties will inevitably fail to measure up, it is more useful to see children's work, both oral and written, as providing an insight into the processes and mechanisms which the children are using. In this way, children's work ceases to be simply 'wrong' and becomes 'data', providing ongoing documentation of the way the child is processing language. The children can themselves be drawn into this view of their own work. Wayne and Matthew, for example, were seriously engaged in the task of analysing their own stories and comparing them to what might have been found in a written text. Once children's work is seen as 'data', rather than as something to be marked 'correct' or 'incorrect', then attitudes of both teachers and pupils can become more positive.

This positive approach is essential for children whose written work has probably brought them little success in the past.

Talk Written Down

The story-telling activity described above can provide the teacher with a range of useful insights into children's language processes. The stories children tell show definite changes as children develop. These changes are not simply the obvious ones of length and vocabulary, but also reflect fundamental differences in use of syntax and awareness of story structure. Compare, for example, the stories told by two 'normal' readers, George, aged seven, and Neil, aged eleven, again in response to a set of picture stimuli.

Once upon a time there was four children and they were called Jack, Jane, Peter and Pam and they phoned up the fire engine people and they came but they realised , the children realised that they didn't need to phone them and they hid but two of the children got caught and the fire engine two men told them off for messing around in telephone boxes. (George)

It all started on Saturday afternoon. Patrick and Rebecca were in a telephone box and they were calling up somebody while Robert and Anne watched with a smile on their face. Then the siren that came with the fire engine came around to help. Then two firemen came out of the fire engine and had a look around and found them. Anne and Robert got away. Unfortunately Rebecca and Patrict were caught and they had a serious word with them. Patrick told the fireman that Rebecca had been phoning up the fire brigade inside the phone box and hid, so that they wouldn't see them and play a joke on them. So the fireman had a word with their parents which got them into more trouble and they went to bed without their tea. (Neil)

Both George and Neil show awareness of the traditional structure of stories, with a definite beginning ('Once upon a time . . . , 'It all started . . . ') and a conclusive end. They both know that stories are generally told in the past tense and they stick firmly to that tense. Both show awareness of cause and effect within the story: both stories have an internal logic which makes sense independent of the picture cards which were the initial story stimulus. Both show an awareness that ambiguity must be clarified in the story-telling process. Neil identifies precisely the subjects of his sentences while George, although less sophisticated, is aware of the need for clarification ('they realised, the children realised').

Where the stories differ most, is in the area of syntax. George uses simple structures similar to those found in the spoken language, with repeated use of 'and' as a chaining device linking parts of his story. Neil, however, uses much more 'literary' language. His story structure is influenced by his awareness of the conventions of the written word. Consequently, he makes much more use of clauses and complex structures ('while Robert and Anne watched . . . ', 'so that they wouldn't see them'). Neil, being older, has been more influenced by the written word, so that his story telling now carries more of the features of written, rather than spoken language. Kress (1982) observed the impact of the structures of written language on children's own writing: it seems that story-telling processes too are affected by what children have read.

Observation of the child's developing skill as a story teller can give useful insight into the processes the child is using. Again, the teacher is acting as observer and data collector. The nature of the data collected can vary from simple length of story, use of vocabulary, to wider questions of story structure, syntax and grammatical usage. Again, while this form of data collection gives useful insight into pupils' development, it can be particularly useful for children with learning difficulties. Compare now the story told by Mike, who, while being the same chronological age as Neil, had a reading age the same as George's.

Richard and Anne are having a conversation because they don't find anywhere to hide they might get caught. And there's Peter and John in the telephone box ringing up the fire brigade and Peter's holding the door open for John because John's a bit small and there's Anne and there's Peter and Anne and there's Jane . . . John . . . and there's Sue getting caught and then there's a man walking along because he wanted to know what was happening because he lives right there and those two are having the argument and the firemen don't know what to do with them so they tell them off and send them home.

We see at once that Mike has little grasp of story structure: his story has no recognisable opening and little logical internal structure. It is heavily dependent on the pictures, and much of it amounts to simple picture by picture identification. On a grammatical level, use of tense is confused and the story slips between past and present. The syntactic structure is simple and makes much use of the simple chaining device 'and'. In fact, Mike's story has much more in common with the sort of stories told by much younger children and reflects his lack of experience with narrative, giving the teacher considerable insight into the kind of work which would benefit him most. He needs exposure to narrative structures through, for example, taped stories and shared reading, and the teacher can modify his programme using the 'data' provided by his story. In this way, the story becomes a tool for diagnosis; it can work in a very similar way to the Informal Reading Inventory, using the child's performance as the basis for future teaching.

Story telling in the classroom

The stories that children tell and record can be used for further teaching, as well as for diagnosis. Once the stories are transcribed, they can form the basis of group work, as they are turned into more formal, recognisable 'written down' structures. Each child in the group should have a copy of every story. The group then works on each story in turn, discussing what changes need to be made in moving from the spoken to the written form. They also have the opportunity to read a range of stories and to offer suggestions for improvements and refinements of plot and characterisation.

The final stage in this editing process is the re-writing of the story in a form acceptable to the original story teller. For many children, especially those with learning difficulties, the final story will be much longer and more complex than they could have managed to write without the help of the story-telling stage and reluctant writers are often surprised by the length and sophistication of their own stories. The exercise enables children who have difficulty in writing to produce more interesting stories, which reflect their ability as language users rather than their technical competence as writers.

There are many possibilities for developing the story-telling process further. In schools with word processors, for example, the teacher might put the transcriptions directly onto the child's file. The subsequent editing process could then be done directly onto the screen and the results printed out.

Writing with a purpose

Approaching writing through the story-telling task gives pupils the experience of successful writing, mediated through the process of transcription. In many ways this approach reflects the 'language experience' approach much used with younger children and adults with literacy problems. When used at a simple level, with the beginning reader of any age, the talk that is written down will probably be very limited. With very young children it may simply be a few sentences which are written down by the teacher as the child is speaking. These sentences will then form the basis of word-recognition exercises and, later, the formation of new sentences. When used in this way, talk becomes the basis of reading: what the child produces may eventually become related to writing through the copying out of the sentences, but the essential focus of the language experience approach is the production of reading material that is of immediate relevance and interest to the person who has produced it.

Where the story-telling approach differs, is in its emphasis on the structure of the narrative produced and its involvement of the pupil in the editing task. The task draws the children's attention to the structure of their own language and encourages a critical appraisal of the language patterns which they already use competently. The stories represent a completed outcome and can be shared with other people. The 'children as authors' approach to writing creates an encouraging environment in which children can see a purpose for their written work. If the stories are well-produced and later illustrated, then the initial story-telling task has linked talking, writing and reading in a coherent and purposeful way.

Keeping up the motivation

Once children have seen the possibilities of producing text in this way, and of relating talking directly to writing, then the task becomes one of maintaining the motivation and positive feeling that 'talk written down' produces. Writing for an audience is one way of maintaining that motivation. For many pupils, an audience of younger children can be the next step in the process of turning talk into print. Writing-resistant children will become enthusiastic when given the chance to write for children at a neighbouring infant school or nursery.

The best story-writing projects start with a field-work visit to the children who are to be the intended audience. Children should be given the opportunity to look at the younger children's books and to discuss with them what kind of stories they like to read. This contact will form an immediate stimulus for ideas and move them on from the initial dependency on the picture stimuli which so far has formed the basis of their story-telling activities. The younger children will suggest a range of possible topics for stories, for example, animals, monsters, space adventure. Once back in their own classroom, the 'writers' will have a great deal of material for discussion. Topics to consider will include the format of children's books, their use of pictures, their repetitions and their talking animals. Once again, talk will be the basis of the stories that are produced. The stories can be produced in a similar way to the earlier sessions. They can be initially 'told' onto the tape-recorder, for later transcription. Alternatively, the teacher might want to write down key words, enabling the child to form complete sentences later.

The editing of such stories will be of prime importance to the children and the necessity for correct spelling and neat presentation will be apparent to all. The stories should be written out on good-quality paper and carefully illustrated. Once completed, the writers should be given the opportunity to return to their intended audience in order to read out their stories. Before the return visit, they should have the opportunity to practise reading, using the tape-recorder.

Once back with the younger children, the relationship of talking and writing is further strengthened for the story writers. They read their stories to small groups of younger children and offer opportunity for discussion. Often the younger children will want to have a go at reading the stories themselves, or will want the 'writers' to read to them from other books. Sometimes, for the first time, the 'writers' have a new status, where their work is appreciated and even admired. Many will ask for a return visit and will be anxious to write more.

Underlying the story-writing project is the sense that writing is a social activity, not an isolated task performed as a chore. It is inextricably bound up with talking as well as with reading and is therefore an activity to which everyone can contribute. The story-telling project can involve children of all abilities and can provide useful opportunities for group work. Extensive use of the tape-recorder will give children confidence and assure them that they have a useful contribution to make.

Extending the Use of Talk

We have been considering the close links that can be forged in the classroom between the activities of talking, writing and reading. It remains finally to consider the important part that parents can play in supporting and extending these links. The role played by parents in their children's school achievement has been increasingly recognised, since the pioneering work of Tizard and others in the early 1980s. Research in many parts of the country has dispelled the myth that only the educated middle classes want to be actively involved in the work their children do at school. Recent evidence suggests that most parents want to be involved, particularly in helping children to read – where social groups differ is simply in their self-confidence. Less educated parents may feel insecure about helping their children, particularly if they are unsure of their own skills. It is here that the teacher can play a significant part in showing parents the benefits of informal, talk-based activities. Tizard and his colleagues suggested that in many ways, time spent helping parents was more useful than time spent on 'remedial' work in the classroom.

Talk, the parent and the teacher

The training of parents in different methods of paired or shared reading can provide many opportunities for encouraging them to make links between talking, reading and writing. The video on shared reading produced in Cleveland County, shows parents that 'reading' with their children can actually consist largely of talking about the books, discussing the pictures and predicting from them what will happen next in the story. Children can be encouraged to tell their own stories based on the pictures in their books: parents are shown that they can help most by encouraging and praising, rather than by correcting inaccurate decoding.

It is this informal, talk-based approach to books that parents often find most difficult to adopt. In a recent project completed in an Oxfordshire school (Boland and Simmons, 1987), one parent said that she avoided discussion when she was helping her child with his reading because 'it delays the agony'. Once parents were introduced to more informal, less corrective approaches, through the use of video and role playing, their responses to helping their children became much more positive. The parents found that they themselves began to enjoy the stories, 'We hadn't noticed the quality before because we were so hung up on word accuracy'. For parents who have little confidence in their own reading ability, the talk-based approach to books can free them from anxiety and enable them to help their children in a pleasurable way.

Increasingly, research suggests that it is not the process of reading itself that helps children who read at home with their parents, but any kind of reading-related activity which seems to lead to positive gains in reading attainment. A small study (Simmons and Loveday, 1987) compared the gain in reading achievements made by children who took part in a shared reading project, with those made by children who played reading games with their parents for a similar length of time. The reading games involved a lot of discussion and provided opportunities for talk between various family members who were invariably drawn into the games for added excitement. Results of the study showed that there were no differences in achievement between the children who had read with their parents and those who had played games. But, interestingly, the parents who had played games with their children felt confident that their children were now doing better with their reading. The games, with their emphasis on talk, had created a positive parent-child rapport and this, in turn, had led to more positive expectations of reading success.

Conclusion

Talk is the starting point for all subsequent learning in the areas of writing and reading. Children are experienced language users when they come to school and teachers can draw on this experience as they introduce children to new skills. For children who experience difficulties in reading and writing, talk provides a natural way-in to other skill areas and provides them with success when they may have become accustomed to failure. Talk can provide a sound starting place for story writing and can enable children to share their ideas with others. No complicated equipment is needed, just a tape-recorder and some opportunity for transcription of the stories. These transcriptions can enable children to become authors and to share their work with a range of other people. Talk is a motivator: when other more formal methods have been unsuccessful, it can give children a start on the road to purposeful writing and reading.

Many of the activities described in this chapter are best suited to individual or small group work. This bias is intentional, since the emphasis of the chapter has been on the unique nature of each child's language development, and on the insight that teachers can gain from gathering 'data' from pupils. However, groups are simply a part of the total classroom picture. How then can such activities fit into the teacher's general classroom structure?

These activities give opportunities for children of varying abilities to work together, either supervised by an adult, or alone with the tape-recorder acting as monitor and guide. Since most of the activities are structured to progress through several stages – talking, transcribing, writing, editing – it is possible to use such outside help at several different points, depending on the children's needs. The talking and writing activities might be seen either as separate enrichment activities for small groups working with an adult, or as an activity in which the whole class is engaged at different stages. Writing for an audience, for example, might well be a teacher-led whole class activity which leads to an appropriate form of public showing. In contrast, a story-telling activity might be designed by the teacher for an individual who needs help, perhaps as an alternative to hearing that child read. Activities can be adapted to be at one time an impetus for the whole group, and at others a diagnostic insight into language behaviour. Underlying all the activities, however, is the sense that in one classroom many different processes are going on at the same time. It is in an attempt to gain knowledge of these processes and to link one with the other that talking and writing can be usefully merged.

References

BOLAND, N. and SIMMONS, K. (1987) 'Attitudes to reading: a parental involvement project, *Education 3-13*, *15*, 2, 29-32.

KRESS, G. (1982) *Learning to Write*. London: Routledge and Kegan Paul.

SIMMONS, K. and LOVEDAY, E. 'Reading: does it matter what parents do?', *Reading*, (in press).

TIZARD, J., SCHOFIELD, W.N. and HEWISON, J. (1982) 'Collaboration between teachers and parents in assisting children's reading', *British Journal of Educational Psychology*, *52*, 1-15.

'Shared Reading' video tape and manual, including a handout for parents, is available from The Education Development Centre, Old Northgate School, Wilton Lane, Guisborough, Cleveland TS14 6JA.

6
Special Needs in Mathematics

Ruth Merttens and Jeff Vass

This chapter sets out a rationale and justification for a particular classroom organisation and associated pedagogy in relation to the maths curriculum. It starts by considering some of the psychological and sociological assumptions which underlie current thinking and research in education, and then outlines a specific mode of classroom organisation, its pedagogy and related mathematical materials and content. We thus attempt to deal both with the theory of special educational needs in the mathematics classroom and with the specific techniques and practices involved.

Background

Perhaps, to mathematics purists, this chapter will cheat. The justification of our approach rests in the belief that maths education and the practice of maths teaching generates a far from 'pure' set of mathematical experiences. We feel this to be true not only in the classroom, but also for sophisticated practitioners of mathematical techniques in the worlds of commerce, industry and science. What do we mean by cheat? Well, when a child has difficulties with maths – number, space, logic, problem solving, etc. – a purist is tempted to look narrowly at the child's behaviour in relation to these specific aspects of mathematics.

Apparently, it is a matter of some amusement for traditional Chinese medics to recall that their western counterparts tend mostly to focus on a particular swelling or pain rather than more general, and to us unconnected, aspects of a patient's life. We can share this amusement. What we see as maths depends on how assessment currently defines it. But this 'school maths' tends to focus on sets of small sub-skills, and specific techniques. We may feel self-congratulatory with the broadening of the curriculum in GCSE maths but this could be premature. The specificity or 'tightness' of a particular mathematical sub-skill is not necessarily changed by making it more practical or more 'in and of the world'. Especially when considering children with learning difficulties, we do well to remember that by extending the time taken to solve a problem by turning it into a practical and supposedly less abstract task, we may well be in danger of stretching the child's ability to maintain the 'sense' of the problem from one moment to the next. And sense, its construction and maintenance, is what really concerns us here in relation to mathematical activity.

Mathematics is full of automatic procedures that have to be acquired, and techniques that have to be mastered. Human beings have to give themselves over to being computers for small amounts of time, to compute or terminate problems once the longer processes of 'making sense' are finished. Yet, because we are human, the question of sense still haunts us in our more automatic modes. Children with 'learning difficulties' are perhaps haunted more than most at such times, often finding it difficult to maintain a sense of the problem through some of the required sub-routines. They often fail to see the relevance of a computation to a problem, even when it seems obvious or self-evident to others.

To get a flavour of this, try the following exercise. We are used to relying upon number bonds in order to perform more complicated addition sums. The sum $2 + 2$ is no sooner written than we look at it and see 4. Take a few minutes right now to sit back and convince yourself that $2 + 2 = 5$.

What happened? Did you really see it? Whether you succeeded or not, try again with this: $2 + 2 = 3$.

Some people see this as pointless, but others admit that they can think themselves into what it might be like to believe it. Some, even some of those who found the whole exercise nonsensical, found $2 + 2 = 3$ easier to believe than $2 + 2 = 5$!

All this should alert us to the capacity of the human mind to be playful even when precise and automatic procedures are demanded. For the able, part of what is needed to perform mathematical skills is the ability to 'switch off' thinking, questioning, playing and wondering, and to switch to automatic. But playing and mental wondering are universal human strategies when one is confronted with a new problem to solve. Perhaps our species found this approach successful in an evolutionary sense, perhaps playing allowed us to alight on solutions by chance.

Already, we have started by placing the actual techniques of problem solving in the context of sense-making. We need, then to turn to the background of this before proceeding on to the classroom and curriculum.

Much of what has already been said here echoes the apparent message of Margaret Donaldson's book *Children's Minds*: the context of learning, even the social context, is crucial to the sense children make of what is required of them and strictly affects their performances. However, one common misinterpretation of Donaldson's book and its message is that a child will find the traditional problems uncharacteristically easier if the context of their presentation is altered, made more familiar, and so on. In other words, if we make the context of learning cosier and more child-centred, then the object of learning is acquired sooner and with less confusion. We feel that this reading of Donaldson is inaccurate. It is useful to look at the structure of the problem-solving situation and classify some points (Figure 6.1).

We have put the various factors involved in mathematical problem-solving in nested brackets rather than in flow-diagram form so as not to privilege one activity over another, and to retain the sense we have of real-world problem solving, which is a continual movement along and through all these factors in the process of solving a problem. Many people tend to think that maths is solely what occurs inside bracket E. Fewer people think of maths as incorporating D and E. Many readers of Donaldson suppose that A and B are independent of C, D and E whilst affecting performance in E, which is, of course, where assessment tends to fix its gaze. Most teachers are aware that much of their time, organisation and energy goes into organising brackets A and B, which remain in the end, hidden. Credit is simply given for performance in E. For children with learning difficulties, though, we feel that assessment would be a fairer enterprise from both the child's and the teacher's point of view if it were to concentrate more heavily on the content of B and C.

If we think of the sorts of problem of a mathematical nature which occur in daily life, on the street and in the home, we become aware of the approximateness of it: '*about* how much

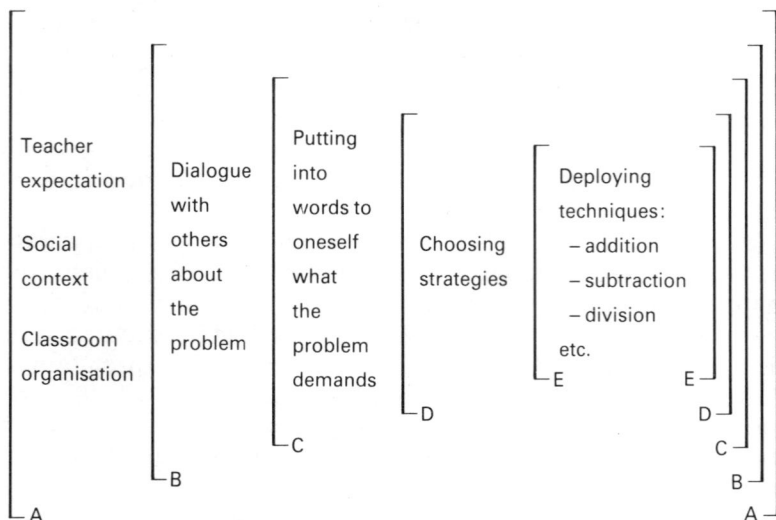

Figure 6.1   Factors involved in mathematical problem solving

money do I take to the shops in order to buy five items for tea?'
'*about* what time do I need to leave home in order to catch the
5.09 train, fitting in a visit to the chemist and the newsagent?'
Finer, detailed planning comes later: 'In what order should I
visit the chemist and newsagent if I need to get to the station
afterwards.' The subtle introduction of the conditional 'if . . . '
indicates a hidden slip into finer and more precise mathematical
thinking. The trouble is that such words still hover in the world
of non-mathematical sense, where such decisions as 'Well, since
I'll probably be less tired tomorrow, I'll go to the chemist then
and not today. I'll sit and have another cup of tea instead' may
take place. Being able to change one's mind and alter plans
seems more a prerogative of life than of mathematics. But
what life offers here, which mathematics sometimes doesn't, is
an image of what the result of such planning and altering will
look like, both in terms of the schedule one will finally adopt
and in terms of what one will experience. One needs a sense of
the 'solution'. Children unable to arrive at such images will fail
to reach the point of choosing strategies and selecting methods.

We need to look more closely at what can be said about the
dialogues, language and choice of strategies that narrowed the

'terminal' activities in maths as described in bracket E. It has been observed (Vygotsky, 1978) that children with recorded IQs of 80 may perform at levels much higher than this would indicate when working with a more able peer group and collaborating on a problem. There is some dispute (Light, 1983) as to whether subsequent individual performance is enhanced when re-tested experimentally. However, one might want to question the design of tests based exclusively on individual performance arising out of strategies developed from individual confrontations with problems. Sharing one's own individual strategies with another often demands that these strategies are made explicit. Even more capable peers may have trouble with this form of sharing. This is probably because such sharing involves itemising one's strategies in language and transmitting them as digestible information.

When two or more children are working together on a problem, a more implicit sharing seems to occur, and the opportunity exists for a more natural acquisition of techniques and skills. Wood *et al.* (1976) speaks of the ever-changing degree of mastery over events once a problem-solving exercise is underway. He points out that two people in the same boat, so to speak, are sensitive to each others' changing degree of mastery and are able to adjust performances to adapt themselves to current developments.

Elsewhere (Vass and Merttens, 1987) we have described other aspects of mathematical problem solving which seem to occur when children are playing a number game where techniques like addition and subtraction are used and being cultivated. Returning to our theme of sense-making in maths, the children observed were immersed in an exploratory dialogue throughout the exercise. Children took various roles in the game so that they each fulfilled different functions in the execution of a problem. One child managed the others, another did some subtracting, another remembered totals, and so on. During the course of the game, the children keenly discussed what the end product should look like and what would constitute 'winning'. In other words, they attempted to generate several images of the solution to the problem solving. Different solutions generated different methods, different ways of playing the game, and different rules and strategies. It seems rather uncontrolled but the situation that developed gave the children opportunities to swap roles; for example, a child could swap functions if he suggested a new end-product.

The result of such dialogue meant that although the children were not all using the same skills and techniques, they were all nevertheless party to what the problem meant in their own terms. Establishing the sense of a problem – what it means – is crucial if children are to be motivated at all. It is worthwhile achieving this, even if it is the more able children who seem to be adopting the more managerial positions in the problem-solving process. By doing this, we are at least able to put the manipulation of learning difficulties back into the sphere of influence of the teacher. If, in group work, one or more children dominate the others and play their 'own' game, this can be remedied by some classroom reorganisation. We refer to this process in more detail later on.

For a class teacher's diagnosis of the 'less able' children in group work, it would be better not to take too much account of the children's performance in the group, which roles they always tend to adopt and so on. Instead encourage such children to teach the game to another child or a group of children who have, as yet, no experience of it. They will thus be forced to take up a managerial responsibility, and will have to set up the process. The teacher can then note the degree to which she has to intervene in order to supplement what the individual child has not yet picked up. Such supplementary information may take the form of the teacher taking an active part in the game. The precise situation may then be clarified – even if a child cannot skilfully deploy a particular technique, the child may at least skilfully manage the moments at which those techniques should be deployed.

Let us now set what has been argued here in the context of a busy classroom and an overburdened curriculum. What are the implications of our case in terms of classroom practice and pedagogy?

With reference to Figure 6.1, we would like to look at some typical problems experienced by teachers of children with learning difficulties when dealing with number work. A teacher will often notice a child who repeats previously 'successful' routines in the forlorn hope that the reapplication of such routines will bring similar success. These children are numerically successful like stopped clocks that are correct twice a day. Although a teacher may be alerted by the child's confusion over which routine to use or which rule to apply, we might be mistaken in concluding that the fault lay somewhere in the D and E region of our diagram.

A child can 'do what was done last time' but still be bewildered by the process involved, even when answers are correct. The child desires to know 'What do I do now?' and 'What do I put?' The separate episodes of solving a problem lack specific meaning and symbols like '+' or '–' are not abstracted as 'techniques'. We have seen a child subtract, by decomposition, pages of sums, i.e.

276 –
179
‾‾‾‾

He would fill in answers in the spaces provided (very often correctly doing the sums mentally) and then go back to the start and, almost at random, put lines through numbers, write in 'carried' numbers etc. to make it all look right.

Immediate sources of difficulty with confusions about processes lie in the child's propensity to be (a) inflexible (and to repeat inapplicable routines) (b) unable to see problems, as distinct from the techniques used to solve them, and (c) someone who guesses, rather than asks, because of an inability to frame the problem in language.

To attempt to deal with such behaviour requires more attention to bracket A of Figure 6.1. What needs to happen is a redistribution of significance at the level at which a problem is framed in language. Rather than make the game one where children correctly complete large numbers of answers, we construct games where choice of strategy constitutes 'successfulness'. The teacher might then pay attention to the forms of peer dialogue that emerge where such games are played with peers, and intervene at the moments where the difficulties we have been discussing are made explicit. Later on, the child will use experience of this dialogue to put questions to herself of the form, 'What can I do with this?' (indicating something tangible and distinct), rather that 'What do I put?'

Sometimes, a teacher will distinguish a child who guesses and is inflexible in number work, from one who presents a general lack of organisation in putting together the elements of a task. This is often correlated with an inability in self-organisation, and a general untidiness resulting from a lack of selectivity, and an inability to follow simple logic. We are now on tricky ground. It is sometimes possible to see playfulness as untidiness.

Some people who live in what looks like an impossible mess often know where to find things. Another's sense of order imposed on the former can have disastrous consequences.

What we are looking for is an inability to order, place and select relevant elements. This amounts to a problem of 'extraction' as opposed to the previous example which was one of 'abstraction'. Psychologists sometimes refer, perhaps unhelpfully, to children with untidy memories and inabilities to store information in hierarchies.

If we return to our theme of making sense of maths in the world, we can see that sorting out elements of a problem can be a gigantic task if we think too microscopically about problem solving. We might give children larger chunks of a problem at a time and pay more attention to the simple logic.

It is important that chunks of a problem have worldly validity rather than 'problem validity'. For example, the number of ways we can express relationships between fractions far exceeds what we can practically do with cakes, teapots and coins. But giving children practice at 'grasping' these chunks and ordering them according to logical principles, is where the teaching might be focused. Again, the organisation of dialogue is of paramount importance here.

'If it takes me 10 minutes to walk a mile; how long will it take me to walk 2 miles?'   [1]

'If it takes 10 minutes to walk a mile; can I walk MORE than 2 miles in 15 minutes?'   [2]

'It takes 10 minutes to walk a mile. In 15 minutes can I walk MORE than 2 miles *or* LESS than 2 miles?   [3]

We will all be aware that presentation of problems is essential when considering approaching children with learning difficulties. In the three examples here, we can point out that the problem is being 'chunked' in various ways. In the first example the basic information is presented, although the second part may leave the child floundering. But it starts with an 'if . . . '; the ' . . . then . . . ' is buried and implicit. This approach depends on a great many skills which we do not normally give credit for.

Example 2 brings out the implicit structure of the problem a bit more. It requires an estimation rather than an actual mathematical solution. The answer is buried in the question and uses part of the answer to chunk the separate elements, i.e. 'MORE'.

Example 3 takes the 'if . . . then' structure completely out. The child chooses a 'more than' or a 'less than' in a different way than in example 2. It gives clues about what the answer looks like, and requires that the child decides what the answer looks like and separates, or 'chunks', the solution from the information required to achieve it. Notice that the second part is a larger piece of language to entertain but it separates at the 'or' rather than the 'more' or the 'less'. In example 2 the 'more' is both part of the problem and a means for chunking it.

Such deliberations over language may seem tortuous, but are necessary when we come to ask how we can teach selectivity to children who demonstrate a lack of order in problem solving.

Classroom Organisation

What is the most helpful structure in the classroom which will enable each child to progress at his or her own rate and will also allow the teacher to cover the mathematical content necessary? How teachers organise the class is, to some extent, dependent upon what materials are available for teaching mathematics. Part of this section is therefore concerned with the use and appropriateness of certain types of schemes and equipment in mathematics.

Group work

The great strength of a good primary classroom lies in the fact that the organisation allows for great flexibility in terms of the children's working environment. Groups of children working together are fluid, rather than being set, and are based on a variety of factors including friendship patterns, interest groups, ability in a particular topic or area, and the different stages of work covered at that time. This allows the teacher much greater control over what the children are doing and also over the amount of group work, as opposed to individual or class work, which takes place.

To organise a classroom in this way requires considerable

initial organisation and planning on the part of the teacher. However, the benefits in terms of both the children's learning and progress, and the reduced stress upon the teacher during the lessons themselves, are immense. It is worthwhile listing briefly those things which we are aiming to achieve through a more flexible classroom structure:

1 Children should have the opportunity to work with a variety of other children. Sometimes this may mean their working with those of widely differing abilities, and at other times in more ability-related groups. However, they do not remain in 'sets'. This not only allows for a wider learning experience for all the children, but it also prevents the worst effects of 'labelling' which occur when children realise that they are in the 'bottom set'.

2 Children should not always be individually responsible for a complete piece of work. They should be encouraged to take collective responsiblity for arriving at a solution or for working through a particular topic. The work may or may not be recorded individually, but decisions will often be joint and should be discussed and argued by all the members of the group.

3 Children should be responsible for the organisation of much more of their work than they usually are. Thus, they may have to decide in what order a series of problems are to be solved, and what actions are necessary, before moving on to the next stage. They may need to select which particular algorithms and procedures are needed in order to obtain the information to enable them to reach a solution to the problem as a whole.

The point about this style of classroom organisation is that it allows the children to develop *all* the strategies necessary for solving problems in the real world. They are not simply concerned with a limited set of algorithms and procedures taken out of context – how to do long-division, how to find the area of a hexagon, or how to construct a graph – but are concerned with the whole process of solving a problem, or a set of problems, from the initial discussions as to how it should be approached, what the solution or solutions might look like and who is going to do what, right through to the addition or subtraction sums which may be needed on the way.

The teacher's role

The role of the teacher becomes rather different when she is not so much concerned with teaching the whole class or with helping individual children through their work cards, as with helping the children to organise their own learning in groups.

First, the teacher has to plan the term's or half-term's curriculum content, and the way it is to be covered, thus deciding which mathematical topics to concentrate on, and in what context they can be set. The teacher then has to plan the structure of the class in terms of the groups in which the children will work. Nevertheless it is often very helpful to introduce a particular topic to the whole class at the same time, so some class teaching may be involved at this stage. Sometimes, at various points throughout a specific piece of work, matters of common or general interest arise and a further class session is called for. Again, at the end it will probably be necessary for each group to report back to the class as a whole, and to conclude with one or two final class lessons.

The teacher must also be aware of the sub-routines that will arise out of any particular topic, and of what these entail. Thus arithmetical skills will be needed for many topics, and spatial awareness or an undertaking of measurement for most. This will be a consideration when putting the children into groups for each particular topic. It will also give an indication of the types of back-up materials which will be needed. If a lot of multiplication is going to be required, then it will be necessary to have plenty of multiplication squares, and perhaps some printed material to practise this, as well as calculators.

Second, the teacher has to make sure that within each group of children working together, each child gets an opportunity to participate. The danger with unsupervised group work is that one or two characters can dominate the group or may do all the work. Alternatively, one child can opt out of the parts of the work that he or she finds difficult or demanding, and make no effort to understand what is going on. Ideally, children learn more effectively from their peers: explanations given by one child to another help not only the child listening, but also the child giving the explanation, since in order to explain something to someone, you have to put it into your own words and hence come to understand it better as a result.

The model for this style of learning, which occurs more

frequently in the primary classroom than in the secondary school, is that of doing homework on the bus going home. For many adults, most of the learning in maths was achieved not in the classroom listening (or not!) to the teacher holding forth, but on the homeward journey, when all the children cooperated and discussed the problems set for homework – 'You don't put an x there, you put it here . . . then you draw a line there . . . I don't se why that should be . . . Well, it's because . . . ' The conversation and discussion which took place on the bus was an invaluable part of coming to understand the mathematics taught in school.

However, as far as possible it is necessary for the teacher to be aware of, and to monitor, the patterns of interaction within each group. Sometimes it will be necessary to set particular individual tasks within the group itself: 'Andrew, you work out the areas involved, and Mary, you find the co-ordinates . . . ' The problems of group work are always much more exaggerated at the beginning. Children do adapt to this style of working and come to realise what is required of them and how they are to behave. At first, they may attempt to abuse the apparent freedom and to use the structure to avoid any productive work. However, generally they do settle and it becomes clearer which particular groupings work, and for what sorts of tasks.

Third, the teacher has to be constantly available for advice, support and help as it is required. Most teaching that goes on will take place within the groups or on an individual basis. A particular problem arises and the teacher's expertise is needed to help the child or children understand how to perform a specific algorithm, or how to approach a particular part of a process.

It is in this context that the teacher needs to have mathematical apparatus or materials available for use as they are required. Sometimes a calculator is appropriate, occasionally it is not because of the need to teach a specific algorithm. Sometimes, if a child is confused about place value, it is best to help individually, perhaps using structural apparatus, while the others in the group are coping with another part of the problem. It is also important to have materials and equipment openly available to all the children in the class. Calculators, computers, squared and graph paper, abaci, counters, Multilink, scales, trundle wheels, measuring equipment, etc., should, in an ideal world, be freely available on demand. In many secondary classrooms this presents a problem, since maths lessons are not always held in the maths room and it becomes necessary to predict in advance what will be required for any particular session. It is possible to do this for the more important or specialised pieces of equipment, but it is difficult to plan for needs which arise spontaneously and often on an individual basis. The only practical solution seems to be for teachers to carry with them a pack of the less expensive and more commonly required equipment, which accompanies them wherever they teach. This can contain things like calculators, squared paper, graph paper, Multilink, tapes or rulers, construction equipment, crayons or felt-tips, glue and so on.

Fourth, the teacher obviously has a role in checking the answers to particular parts as they arise, and diagnosing when things are going wrong in time for action to be taken. Sometimes it seems as if we are asking children to re-invent the wheel! Teacher assistance at a crucial point can prevent frustration and ultimately a lot of boredom. Although the teacher will probably do less 'marking' of work as such, she does need to pick up mistakes, especially those that are recurring as a result of a misunderstanding, so that the children can be helped. At times, it may also be advisable to ask a particular group of children, or even the whole class, to practise a specific procedure, and then to check how successfully they have coped. But this type of work should remain occasional and should not be allowed to take over from the main thrust of the more context-based problem-solving activity which forms the basis for the group's work.

Finally, the teacher also has to be able to suggest ways of extending any particular area of work so that all the children remain stimulated and involved. Sometimes, several groups can be working on the same problem, but employing different techniques and taking it in different directions according to their abilities. Once again, this is commonplace in the primary classroom, but more unusual in the secondary school. Extension materials can be exceedingly useful in this context, since even the most inventive teacher cannot be expected to generate new ideas and extensions day after day in all the areas of mathematics in which she teaches!

The Mathematics Curriculum

It is important that children, especially those with learning difficulties, are able to make sense of the whole problem and to maintain that 'sense' continuously throughout the whole of the problem-solving process. This will enable them to plan the use of sub-routines and strategies and to organise how to proceed. To enable children to maintain this 'sense' of a problem it is helpful to set the mathematics in a meaningful context as far as possible. However, sometimes this stretches the imagination and the children's credulity to breaking point. It is far better to take a maths topic, such as solving solutions, and to explore it in a variety of interesting ways – graphical, algebraic, using matrices, etc. – than to force a situation in which particular equations 'arise'. It is important to remember that a 'topic' can be a mathematical one.

Relevance, for children (and for adults), is not the same thing as immediate usefulness. Teenage children will play for hours on role-playing games which have no use-value but which fascinate them endlessly and which incorporate and demand all sorts of specific mathematical skills, such as the manipulation of percentages, ratios and probability. What must be continually borne in mind is not so much the usefulness of a particular piece of maths, since children will put energy into all sorts of 'useless' pursuits, but its ability to hold the children's interest and concentration throughout. This will enable them to maintain a notion of the whole problem whilst they are having to negotiate and deploy sub-skills and intermediate strategies.

However, it is also important that children, especially those with special educational needs, acquire the life skills necessary to operate fully within society as it is presently constructed. Thus, there should be an emphasis on setting the mathematical content of the curriculum into a context which makes it clear and relevant. Topic work obviously has a crucial role to play in this, and it is surprising how different the skills are that are required to estimate or measure something in real life, than to perform a paper and pencil calculation on measurement. Given the requirements of assessment, children need to have experience of both. Thus, for example, they should be able to measure out 15 cc of a medicine composed of a ratio of two to one, medicine to water, and to do a calculation which will give the relative proportions in figures on a page.

Materials

Many of the materials for both secondary and primary schools are unfortunately designed with individualised learning principally in mind. Thus, the children are asked to work through a series of cards or booklets, on a largely individual basis. This trend was motivated by the desire to allow children of a wide range of mathematical ability to work through the curriculum at their own pace. However, it has had several unfortunate and largely unforeseen effects upon children's learning. First, it completely removes the 'doing homework together and discussing what went on' syndrome mentioned earlier. Children plodding through their own cards at their own level are unable to share their struggles and learning with others. The individual approach ignores the fact that, as mentioned earlier, dialogue plays an important part in the learning process. Secondly, it makes it more difficult to organise meaningful and relevant class sessions. Some teachers attempt to get round this by doing a regular 'class investigation'. However, this only partly solves the problem, since many children perceive these investigations as peripheral to the 'real maths learning'. Also, although the investigation may be set for the whole class, by and large the children, especially the more able and the less able, tend to approach the investigation on an individual basis, if only because they are used to working in that way. The other major drawback with the individualised learning schemes is that they emphasise the differences between the children, both in terms of how fast they can progress and in the mathematical content they are capable of tackling at any specified moment.

The alternative to individualised learning has too often been seen in the past to be 'old-fashioned' class teaching. This has meant a false dichotomy between child-centred individualised learning schemes on the one hand, and teacher-centred formal class lessons on the other. In practice we are looking to develop much more group work and to enable peer-group interaction to take place, at the same time as situating the mathematical content of the curriculum within a more meaningful and less isolated context.

It is therefore important to search out those materials, whether they are books or cards, which allow the imposition of a classroom structure as described above. This may well involve a mixture of materials, some from one source, some from another, and some teacher-written materials. It will certainly involve teachers in a careful planning of the term's or half-term's work, both in terms of content and the materials necessary. However, as many primary class teachers have found, this type of planning and organisation pays huge dividends, not only in terms of the children's learning and enthusiasm, but also in terms of reducing teacher anxiety and pressure later in the term.

Record-keeping

The children can, in part, be responsible for their own record-keeping. Each group can be asked to keep a written record of its work, and also to display the group's solutions as and when it achieves them. Groups can be required to think how best to display the information so that it is readily accessible. This will involve them in some thought about graphical and pictorial representation, as well as in written work and tabulations.

A system of working which involves group work, calls for fairly tight record-keeping and assessment on the part of the teacher. After each topic, it is necessary to keep a record of what each individual child covered, mathematically speaking, and to make some judgment about what each child got out of it. These records do not need to be lengthy, but they do need to be complete. A system of coding saves time and a sort of check list drawn up at the same time that the initial planning for that topic takes place may be very helpful. Sometimes one sentence on the child's record can help a great deal in being able to monitor his or her progress when looking back over a series of pieces of work.

Conclusion

In conclusion, let us acknowledge the importance and difficulties associated with what we are saying. If a child with learning difficulties is approaching abstract work, but has not mastered the language or skills of spatial relations, then one may be best advised to take the child aside and do some spatial awareness exercises.

However, such advice, while appropriate and well-intentioned, is not perhaps rooted in the busy classroom. We are suggesting that teachers might make a 'deal' with conditions, as they find them, and utilise mixed-ability teaching to the advantage of children with learning difficulties.

Our suggestions are geared to pointing the educator's attention to the circumstances in which children can cultivate global and cooperative strategies toward mathematical tasks, where these children typically come unstuck before they start.

We began by stressing the importance of situating mathematical sub-routines in contexts where sense can be made of them. Many learning difficulties are located in those contexts rather than in the sub-routines. When we can locate these difficulties, we can find pathways through a flexible classroom structure which allows remediation at the level of organisation, of talk and activity, rather than in the execution of precise skills.

Above all, classroom structure should reflect, and indeed foster, the degree of flexibility and play we always have and must continue to bring to the world in order to solve the problems we are presented with in everyday life. Not terribly radical ideas when you think that the structure of human learning has been based on these principles for about four million years.

References

DONALDSON, M. (1978) *Children's Minds.* Glasgow: Fontana.

LIGHT, P.(1983) 'Review of post-Piagetian research' in MEADOWS, S. *Developing Thinking: Approaches to Children's Cognitive Development.* London: Methuen.

VASS, J. and MERTTENS, R. (1987) 'The cultural mediation and determination of intuitive knowledge and cognitive development' in Proceedings of the Sixth Conference on Child Development: 'Growing in the Modern World'. 10–13 June, 1987, Trondheim, Norway.

VYGOTSKY, L.S. (1978) *Mind in Society: The Development of Higher Psychological Processes.* Cambridge: Harvard University Press.

WOOD, D., BRUNER, J.S. and ROSS, G. (1976) 'The role of tutoring in problem solving', *Journal of Child Psychology and Psychiatry, 17,* 89-100.

7
Behaviour Difficulties: School Policy and Classroom Management

John Dwyfor Davies and Pat Davies

Many children with behaviour difficulties in school frequently exhibit an uncanny ability to manipulate circumstances to suit their needs (Dockar-Drysdale, 1967). They are often adept at manipulating adults, discovering weaknesses and using these to their own ends.

Traditionally, teachers have assumed responsibility for their own class groups and, with it, have accepted the need to resolve any difficulties in a way that they feel is appropriate. The difficulty with such an approach, however, is that for many teachers, coping with disruptive pupils will inadvertently involve them in either a power struggle for order and control, or in colluding with the pupil. In the extreme, this will leave the teacher further exposed to the will of the pupil, who then assumes covert, if not overt control in the classroom setting. Such a situation is potentially damaging for the individual teacher, the child and the school as a whole.

It has, until recently, been assumed that the school could do little to affect the behaviour of its pupils. The influence of the home and parental modelling was regarded as so significant that the school could do little to counter it. More recently, research by Reynolds, (1976), Rutter *et al.* (1979), Mortimore (1986) and others, suggest that this is by no means the case. The school does have a direct influence on the behaviour exhibited by its pupils, irrespective of home background or individual ability.

In this context, a school policy is needed which supports individual teachers, respects pupils' individuality and is consistently applied. Galloway and Goodwin (1987) suggest that:

. . . the most effective procedures for preventing, rather than treating, disturbing . . . behaviour are a by-product of processes which aim to raise the overall quality of education for *all* pupils in the school . . . In general, schools which cater successfully for their most disturbing pupils *also* cater successfully for the rest of their pupils.

Effecting a whole school policy, however, is a highly complex and difficult exercise (Thomas and Jackson, 1985). In practice, the task is complicated by the fact that teachers are faced with considering ways of effecting a preventative policy, on three separate levels simultaneously:

1 At school level;
2 At group and classroom level; and
3 At the level of individual management.

At School Level

The ethos of the school

As already noted, recent research has started to highlight the part played by schools in creating or minimising the degree of behaviour difficulties they experience. Reynolds (1987) has summarised the eight most significant factors as:

1 High teacher expectation of pupil ability, irrespective of home background.
2 Emphasis on academic achievement.
3 Strong leadership which effectively communicates with staff and subsequently involves them in decision making. Thereafter devolving certain responsibilities to individual staff members.
4 Good, supportive interpersonal relations amongst the staff team.
5 Parental involvement in the life of the school and good relationships with the local community.
6 Student involvement in the life of the school.
7 Emphasis on reward rather than punishment.
8 A clear policy and consistency of application of rewards and punishment.

Similar factors have again been identified as significant by the study in London primary schools (Mortimore, 1986). These findings suggest that:

- strong leadership,
- involvement of the entire staff in the implementation of policy;
- strong focus on educational objectives;
- pupil and parent participation,

all further the goal of developing a positive school ethos.

The school in the community – presenting an image

The image a school presents is important and should not be underestimated for several reasons, all of which may well be influential in arriving at a positive climate that is conducive to preventing behaviour difficulties becoming established. The fostering of closer links with, and participation by, parents can be helped when they perceive the school as a warm and welcoming place. In contrast, a barren, hostile appearance is more likely to hinder these developments by inhibiting parents and other members of the community from wanting to enter the school and from associating directly with it. It is reassuring that some local authorities are now placing a greater importance on this and attempting to find ways of encouraging their schools to become more welcoming and accessible to parents. Oxfordshire, for example, has recently appointed a team of five advisory headteachers, with the sole brief to develop community links within schools. It has also made money available to enable schools to develop a more positive image.

From the pupil perspective, the same is likely to be true. Rutter (1979) suggests that one of the significant factors within the more successful schools was the lack of graffiti, symbolising an environment that was well cared for and one which presented a pleasant setting in which to work. Bettelheim (1950) has long recognised the importance of the environment and its effect on behaviour. In ignoring this aspect of our schools, we may well be contributing to the negative ethos that we wish to diminish.

At Group and Classroom Level

Enhanced understanding of individual children can be furthered not only through closer collaboration between home and school, but also as a result of a pastoral structure within the school which enables the teacher to become actively involved in work that helps the pupil acquire a growing knowledge of him/herself. The development of active tutorial work in many secondary schools over recent years, is one example of how this can be achieved. For it to be effective, we must move away from the notion that pastoral work is a separate entity, to be considered only at times designated for tutorial work. It is when pastoral work is seen as a thread which permeates the whole life of the school, that it is likely to have maximum effect. Galloway and Goodwin identify several distinct ways in which this can be achieved.

1 Enhanced involvement by form tutors, in tracking the academic work of individual pupils. Regularly ensuring that homework is completed, for example, may enable the teacher to identify pupils who are beginning to experience difficulties. In this way, a dialogue can be established before that pupil becomes totally disaffected with school and remedial action adopted.
2 Adopting strategies that keep parents closely in touch with and aware of what is happening at school, in such a way that they are invited to participate and comment on their child's progress and development informally and regularly.
3 The use of tutorial periods to involve pupils directly in exercises that help them to develop their self-esteem and to develop a growing understanding of the role of the school and their part within this.
4 Through tutorial work, pupils can begin to develop increased understanding and tolerance of individual differences in a way that cannot be assumed if left to chance.

This has clear implications for a whole school policy, since (a) it can only be effective if such a programme is designed as an integral aspect of the life of the school and (b) it operates throughout the pupil's school career. Neither can be achieved unless the entire staff are committed to such a policy and work jointly to effect it. Whilst the adoption of such approaches can help individual teachers gain increased insight and understanding of pupils in their care, much would be wasted if important information is not transmitted to other key members of staff. The implication here is that a whole school approach necessitates the development of a structure that can ensure effective communication between teachers. This involves a far wider and more coherent pathway than can be left to chance. It is not adequate to assume that this information will be conveyed through casual and informal interchange between staff members.

Communication in a large school is never easy, and it is therefore necessary to find ways of minimising the breakdown of vital information reaching key staff. Many schools have already identified one or more members of staff whose role includes that of coordinating the school's pastoral work – ensuring that colleagues are kept informed about individual pupils so that cohesive action can be taken.

Research again suggests that good interpersonal relations amongst the staff are important if the school is to be effective in minimising disruption (Reid, Hopkins and Holly, 1986). Similarly, a commitment from the staff to achieve specified goals has been found to be significant. However, when Rouse (1982) asked the staff of six comprehensive schools to rank in order the forms of behaviour that they regarded as most indicative of misbehaviour, she found that there was no correlation between individuals as to what was regarded as most significant. In fact, what emerged was the wide dissimilarity of view between individuals as well as between schools. To effect a greater degree of cohesion, structures need to be established through which the staff, as a whole, can discuss and finally arrive at standards and expectations that represent a consensus.

Establishing a climate that is both positive and constructive is important to the task of preventing disruption (Bayliss, 1986). To this end, an emphasis on rewarding positive behaviour can be highly motivating for pupils and a powerful means of establishing a positive climate (Reid, Hopkins and Holly, 1986). Yet, in practice, this is far less evident than the tendency to focus on negative behaviour. In her study, Rouse (1982) found that when questioned about the use of rewarding good behaviour, the vast majority of schools rarely used positive rewards. Furthermore, public praise for improvement and good behaviour was used less often than individual acknowledgment such as letters to parents or the awarding of house points to pupils. Webb (1987) came to similar conclusions in researching behaviour management in the primary sector.

Punctuality – a keystone to success

The climate of any lesson is established long before it actually gets underway. Within the first few minutes after a group of pupils has entered a classroom, the tone is set. Consequently, it is important that the teacher does not allow the group to create an environment which is not conducive to appropriate behaviour. Ideally, this implies that the teacher is waiting to receive the group and, while monitoring entry to the classroom, is able to modify inappropriate interaction between pupils (Partington and Hinchliffe, 1979). Whilst in practice, it is not always possible to be in a classroom before the first pupils arrive – particularly in a secondary school where the teachers as well as the pupils may have to move between classrooms – it is vitally important that a group is not left unattended for too long at the start of a lesson. Punctuality, then, is a keynote if the potential for disruption is to be minimised. Allied to this, is the need to ensure that the group is aware of the expectations that are to be made of it.

Clear expectations

It cannot be assumed that each individual will be familiar as to what is expected, in terms of behaviour or achievement. It may be helpful to clarify this point at the start of a lesson and to reinforce it, as necessary, thereafter. Uncertainty as to the limits to which a teacher will allow behaviour to develop may well lead to individuals or groups of children adopting a 'testing out' stance in an attempt to establish this for themselves. Within such a situation, the potential for disruption is increased and the teacher's task complicated.

Smooth activity flow

Kounin (1970) has noted the kinds of teacher behaviour that can aid and hinder the effective management of behaviour in groups, and suggests that it is important for teachers to demonstrate an ability to identify the source of disruption *before* it escalates so as to intervene quickly and effectively. Equally, it is important that any intervention is directed at the pupil responsible for the disruption. Too frequently, the instigator has withdrawn from the scene of conflict by the time the teacher has noted it and the ensuing intervention is directed at another child, who may well be reacting to the initial provocation. This can lead to a feeling of injustice by the recipient of such a response and do little to help in the long term.

The ability therefore, to show a quality that Kounin describes as 'withitness' is a great asset to the teacher. By informing a pupil that this behaviour is noted, while continuing with another task, will not only alert the individual but the whole class group to the fact that the teacher is aware of potential disruption. In the same way, an ability to 'overlap', can aid in the process of ensuring a smoother flow to the lesson. By this, Kounin is referring to the ability to attend to more than one task at a time, and by so doing, again intervening at a timely point.

Avoiding the tendency to dwell on details that the group has clearly understood can help prevent restlessness. Equally important in maintaining a high degree of activity flow is the avoidance of 'overemphasis', 'dangling' and 'flip-flops', by which Kounin refers to the tendency to start an activity but then allow it to 'dangle' whilst attending to something else; and starting an activity, stopping it to attend to a previous activity and then again returning to the original activity. Kounin also showed that disruptive behaviour could be reduced by the teacher using alerting cues, for example, 'Someone else will be asked to carry on reading from where Mark stops' and accountability cues, for example, 'You will be expected to show your completed work to the rest of the class at the end of the lesson'. This is very much in line with more recent work referred to above which again helps restate the high degree of expectations made on pupils and has been found to be helpful in establishing and maintaining a positive and constructive ethos.

Along with Jones (1976), Kounin emphasises the effect of boredom on pupils and the tendency for disruption to occur when an activity or task has lost its interest for individuals. At the same time, it can be equally disruptive to the activity flow, if pupils are offered too much choice of activity or materials (Bayliss, 1986).

Promoting group cohesion

Johnson and Bany (1970) emphasised the importance of developing and promoting group cohesion. Teachers who actively sought to achieve this were seen as more successful in limiting behaviour problems than those who did not. Favourable group appraisal, the avoidance of group criticism, relaying to the class positive remarks and comments from other teachers or visitors, classroom activities involving the whole group in a joint planning exercise and implementing the ideas together, were all found to be useful strategies in promoting group cohesion.

At an Individual Level

Much of what has been discussed above has drawn attention to the value of increasing positive interaction between teacher and pupil. The more that is known and understood about individual pupils, the more likely it is that the teacher can act in ways that will minimise disruptive behaviour. At the level of individual interaction in the classroom, several factors have been found to be significant. Redl (1957) has itemised a range of strategies available to teachers when confronted with disruptive behaviour from individual pupils. The effectiveness of most of these assumes a high degree of respect and understanding by the teacher of the child's needs:

Planned ignoring – This assumes that the teacher is both aware of the overt behaviour a child is exhibiting and of possible *reasons* for that behaviour. Armed with this knowledge, the teacher is able to make a decision to ignore, rather than to re-inforce it negatively. Clearly, planned ignoring is not the same as overlooking the behaviour simply because the teacher is at a loss as to how to react. Such a strategy need not imply complete ignoring. Laslett and Smith 1984) have pointed out that a teacher may well ignore provocative behaviour, only to return to it later when the child is in a more receptive frame of mind.

Signal interference – Allied to planned ignoring is signal interference. This strategy involves making a pupil aware of the fact that the teacher knows what is happening and disapproves of it, but again without reinforcing the negative behaviour. This can be achieved by catching the pupil's eye, and by the facial expressions conveying a firm message to the pupil. In the same way, the use of other forms of body language by a teacher can be equally effective in signalling disapproval to the child.

Proximity and touch control – The simple act of placing a hand gently on the shoulder of a pupil who may well be involved in the early stages of a disruptive activity, can often help deflate a potentially difficult situation. Again, this can alert the individual to the fact that the teacher is aware of the situation, disapproves and has alerted the pupil to the fact. It should be stressed that in no way is this the same as physical intervention. Indeed, much classroom confrontation may well be the result of a teacher's intervention which is interpreted as threatening by the pupil.

Involvement in interest relationship – Knowing the individual well enough to be aware of special areas of interest can often be of assistance to the teacher. In this way, material can be prepared, or activities planned that can relate to these special interests. Far from 'giving in' to a difficult child, such flexibility on the part of the teacher is a recognition of considerable professional skill.

Affection – The expression of genuine warmth by the teacher can often be a powerful influence in preventing a difficult situation escalating still further. Here again, such intervention is most effective when the teacher knows the context in which the behaviour is being exhibited and knows the child concerned well enough to be sure that the affection shown will be understood and accepted.

Humour – A sense of humour is not only a lifeline for the teacher under stress, but it can be used positively to defuse conflict situations, particularly in the early stages of their development. It is important, however, that humour is not confused with sarcasm which could help fan the flames of early confrontation, whilst at the same time considerably reducing the pupil's confidence in and respect for the teacher.

Hurdle help – Often, disruptive behaviour arises as a result of a pupil becoming increasingly frustrated and restless through inability to negotiate a set task successfully. The teacher's knowledge of individuals within the group who are likely to find aspects of set tasks difficult, can lead to appropriate help being offered to these pupils, before the frustration sets in.

Interpretation – Disruption can sometimes result from a pupil misunderstanding or misinterpreting the action of another. The accidental bump by one child as he passes another may be seen as a threatening gesture that has to be responded to. In such a situation, it can often help if the teacher is able to interpret the interaction and through explanation, prevent the problem escalating.

Regrouping – It is not perhaps surprising that some children will not work or interact socially together. Different personalities sometimes have trouble tolerating one another. In other circumstances, rivalry between individuals may have a long history, perhaps involving family feuds and where this is the case, disruption may be prevented if certain individuals are not placed in the same group to work.

Restructuring – Heightened knowledge of the group, of individuals within the group *and* of the subject matter involved in a particular lesson, can help a teacher who is able to note a degree of restlessness which may be caused by the structure of the lesson. The ability to act flexibly and to restructure the nature or content of the lesson may again prevent a disruptive situation developing.

Direct appeal – For some pupils, it will be enough if the teacher makes a direct appeal for improvement in their behaviour. For this to be effective however, the teacher will again need to know the pupil concerned very well and to be sure that the pupil holds enough respect for the teacher to make use of such a tactic.

Limitation of space and tools – When working with some pupils, it may be necessary to limit the space in which they are operating and the choice of materials at their disposal, as some children experience considerable difficulty, both in making choices and in structuring their environment. In such circumstances, limiting their mobility and reducing the stimulus to which they are exposed, together with the choices available to them, may help reduce the potential for disruption.

Time out – Under certain circumstances, it may be necessary to withdraw a child from a scene of conflict and to allow him or her the space in which to regain composure, and a balanced focus on a difficult situation. Much has been written on this subject (Herbert, 1981), but the practical application of such a technique may present difficulties for some mainstream schools.

Contracts – Some pupils find difficulty in maintaining positive behaviour without a concrete structure to support them. For such children, the use of contracts may prove useful. Contracts may be drawn up through discussion between teacher and pupil, in which agreed patterns of behaviour are arrived at. These are stipulated in writing and jointly signed. Their value lies in the fact that the pupil feels that she/he had some say in the agreement and consequently has an investment in it. It is therefore more likely that the desired behaviour will be maintained (Epenchin and Paul, 1982). Epenchin and Paul identify five important elements which should be included in such a contract:

1 A clear description of the desired behaviour.
2 A description of the reward for the compliance.
3 How the contract will be monitored.
4 When the contract will be negotiated.
5 Signatures of all involved.

It may also include a clause which states what the pupil will receive if he does particularly well and another to specify what might be the result of defying the contract.

Avoiding negative strategies

As well as those strategies that have been found to be positive when used by teachers, others tend to escalate disruptive behaviour and should be carefully avoided. Public reprimand, which draws further attention both to the behaviour and the individual concerned, serves little use, other than to confirm in the child's mind that the teacher is in a position to abuse his or her superior position. Laslett and Smith (1984) suggest that such form of teacher response is essentially bullying and is likely to instil much the same resentment in children as physical bullying. Meighan (1978) concludes that children do not mind teachers being strict, but they have no respect for those who are nasty or sarcastic.

Teacher/Parent Partnership – The New Orthodoxy

The importance of home/school partnership and the way that this affects children's learning is well documented (Halsey, 1972; Tizard and Hughes, 1984). A realistic, meaningful relationship however, is not always easy to achieve, but despite the difficulty of the task, sound links need to be forged so that communication is facilitated between the two parties. Schools which adopt a cooperative, rather than a patronising approach to this task, are likely to be more effective. Tizard and Hughes (1984) emphasise the need for the sensitive implementation of any collaborative policy. 'Almost all parents respond with interest when someone knowledgeable shows an individual concern for their child and points out to them aspects of their development which they had been unaware of.'

When parents become convinced of the value of their own contribution, feelings of helplessness, despair and guilt which may have compounded their child's feeling of failure, can be harnessed, with a profound growth in self-esteem, leading to increased responsibility and motivation. It is the interaction between parent and teacher, based on an open and professional understanding that can generate mutual respect which enables a growth of understanding of the child's behaviour. From this can emerge patterns of working with the child that are informed and meaningful, rooted in sound knowledge of individual differences and acknowledging the meaning underpinning the overt behaviour.

School Based In-service

If attitudes are not only to be modified, but also continually reviewed in the light of developments within the school and the community, it may be necessary to implement a programme of in-service training which is school-based and school-focused. It is no coincidence that recent developments in in-service education for teachers have shifted from the traditional college-based, long-term secondment model, to a more school-based, continuous one. Government initiatives on this front have meant that it is now possible to effect more efficient programmes that can more readily achieve the aims identified above (Simmons 1987). At the same time, the development in the focus of in-service work has stimulated educationists such as Grunsell (1985) and Amphlett *et al.* (1986) to produce material that can be modified to meet the in-service needs of individual schools and which invites the staff of such schools to look critically at the provision presently offered and at ways to refine it. This form of in-service provision is designed so that the entire staff of a school can begin to find ways of translating the research findings into practice.

Conclusion

From the teacher's point of view, it may be necessary to remember that in working with children who are likely to present behaviour problems, the positive, preventative approach is always better than one which involves the teacher in searching for remedial action after disruption has occurred. Yet in practice, this is not always easy to achieve. Whilst the techniques identified in this chapter can all be seen as useful, there is no firm rule which helps the teacher to select the most appropriate strategy. No two situations are identical and no two pupils the same. It calls on the professional skill of the teacher to select the proposed action to suit each particular situation. This is why a detailed understanding of the individual child concerned can help greatly in the task of selecting the most appropriate form of action. In this knowledge, it is likely that the chance of mis-matching the response to the behaviour can be minimised. Research is beginning to indicate general areas that need to be taken seriously in the search for a more supportive school climate. The collective determination of the whole staff, with a coordinated response, involving the head, staff, pupils and parents alike, is all important.

References

AMPHLETT, D., DAVIES, J.D. and JONES, D. (1986) *In the Heat of the Moment*. Oxford: Oxford Polytechnic Press.

BAYLISS, S. (1986) 'Twelve rungs on the ladder to success' *Times Educational Supplement*, 5 April 1986.

BETTELHEIM, B. (1950) *Love is Not Enough*. Glencoe, Illinois: Free Press.

DOCKAR-DRYSDALE, B. (1967) *Consultation in Child Care*. Harlow: Longman.

EPENCHIN, B.C. and PAUL, J.L. (1982) *Casebook for Educating the Emotionally Disturbed*. London: Merrill Publishing International.

ERIKSON, E.H. (1965) *Childhood and Society*. Middlesex: Penguin Books.

GALLOWAY, D., BALL, T., BLOMFIELD, D. and SEYD, R. (1982) *Schools and Disruptive Pupils*. Harlow: Longman.

GALLOWAY, D. (1982) 'A study of pupils suspended from schools, *British Journal of Educational Psychology*, 52, 205-12.

GALLOWAY, D. and GOODWIN, C. (1987) *The Education of Disturbing Children: Pupils with Learning and Adjustment Difficulties*. Harlow: Longman.

GILLHAM, B. (1981) *Problem Behaviour in the Secondary School*. Beckenham: Croom Helm.

GRUNSELL, R. (1985) *Finding Answers to Disruption: Discussion Exercises for Secondary Teachers*. Harlow: Longman.

HALSEY, A.H. (1972) *Educational Priority – EPA Problems and Policies*. London: HMSO.

HERBERT, M. (1984) *Behaviour Treatment of Problem Children*. London: Academic Press.

HEWETT, F.H. (1979) *The Emotionally Disturbed Child in the Classroom*. London: Allyn & Bacon.

JOHNSON, and BANY, (1970) *Classroom Management: theory and skill training*. Middlesex: Collier Macmillan.

JONES, A. (1977) 'Disruptive pupils in the secondary school' in JONES-DAVIES, C. and CAVE, R. (eds) *The Disruptive Pupil in the Secondary School*. London: Ward Lock Educational.

KOUNIN, J.S. (1970) *Discipline and Group Management in Classrooms.* Eastbourne: Holt, Rinehart and Winston.

LASLETT, R. and SMITH, C. (1984) *Effective Classroom Management.* Beckenham: Croom Helm.

MORTIMORE, P. (1986) *The Junior School Project: A Summary of the Main Report.* Inner London Education Authority.

PARTINGTON, J.A. and HINCHLIFFE, G. (1979) 'Some Aspects of Classroom Management', *British Journal of Teacher Education, 5, 3,* 231-41.

POTTS, P. (1983) 'Summary and prospect' in BOOTH, T. and POTTS, P. (eds) *Integrating Special Education.* Oxford: Basil Blackwell.

REDL, F. (1957) *The Aggressive Child.* USA: Free Press.

REID, K., HOPKINS, D. and HOLLY, P. (1986) *Towards the Effective School.* Oxford: Basil Blackwell.

REYNOLDS, D. (1976) 'When pupils and teachers refuse a truce; the secondary school and the creation of delinquency' in MUNGHAM, G. and PEARSON, G. (eds) *Working Class Youth Culture.* London: Routledge and Kegan Paul.

REYNOLDS, D. (1987) 'School effectiveness and truancy' in REID, K. (ed.) *Combating School Absenteeism.* London: Hodder and Stoughton.

ROUSE, C. (1982) *Standards of Behaviour in Secondary Schools.* Oxford: Oxford Polytechnic, School of Education. Unpublished.

RUTTER, M., MAUGHAN, B., MORTIMORE, P. and OUSTON, J. (1979) *Fifteen Thousand Hours: Secondary Schools and their Effect on Children.* London: Open Books.

SIMMONS, K. (1987) 'A new partnership?', *Times Educational Supplement,* 11 September.

THOMAS, G. and JACKSON, B. (1985) 'The whole school approach', *The British Journal of Special Education, 13,* 1, 17-24.

TIZARD, B. and HUGHES, M. (1984) *Young Children Learning.* London: Fontana.

TOMLINSON, S. (1983) *Professionals and ESN(M) education* in SWANN, W. (ed.) *The Practice of Special Education.* Oxford: Basil Blackwell.

WEBB, C.A.M. (1987) *Behaviour Management in Primary Schools.* Oxford: Oxford Polytechnic School of Education, Unpublished Dissertation.

WIDLAKE, P. (1986) *Reducing Educational Disadvantage.* Milton Keynes: Open University Press.

Conclusion

Warnock and the 1981 Act have coincidentally been framed at a time of great change in society. Only ten years before the Act, Touraine (1971) was talking of the coming of a 'post-industrial society'. Such a society is now conspicuously with us. It is perhaps fortuitous that the questions such changes in society force on education coincide with a time of questioning and reappraisal for special needs – for the two sets of questions are linked. It could be argued that many of today's children, often those identified as having special needs – the truants, the disaffected, the 'low attaining pupils' – are hostile to the idea of school because they see no relevance in it. Often pupils are switched off from school because the curriculum in its tight compartments, and school organisation with its emphasis on the maintenance of authority are still geared towards the needs of nineteenth-century industrial society – not those of the post-industrial society. This is not to say that society's needs have to provide the impetus for changes in education, rather it is to suggest that there has to be a process of continuous reappraisal of the goals of education if we are to do our best for the children in our charge. It becomes increasingly clear that if there is to be success in providing an appropriate education for *all* children, attention needs to be focused on two central areas: school organisation in the form of pastoral and support systems, and curriculum change and development.

Defining the Special Curriculum

At present, assessment is a powerful force in shaping the curriculum both in special and in mainstream education. Assessment in special needs in the traditional norm-referenced mould (using, for example, IQ tests) often took the form of merely determining placement in a particular kind of special school or class within a mainstream school. Its development into a kind of diagnostic tool in the 1970s has been criticised as ineffective because it placed the focus inappropriately on the child's weaknesses rather than on the suitability or presentation of materials and teaching methods. Further development from this into criterion-referenced instruments, while widely applauded, inevitably identified the same set of children while doing nothing about the curriculum, systems or practices which labelled the children as special. The question needs to be asked, 'Are these children in special need because of what the system requires them to do?' It is an irony that the newer criterion-referenced assessment, which is supposed to be curriculum-based, is in fact the reverse: it is not so much curriculum-based assessment as assessment-based curriculum, and has been a powerful force in shaping the curriculum and maintaining the status quo.

Taking a wider look at mainstream education, we find that many of the processes which are being attacked as damaging to the development of better practice in special education – such as assessment – in fact occur throughout the system. Much of the curriculum of children in secondary schools is geared around achievement at examinations, and it is wholly inappropriate that a model such as this should structure the way in which we formulate the curriculum for children who have been identified as having special needs. It might be argued, however, that the curriculum is not formulated in this way, and that the examinations and curricula which arise from them, are in no way related to the curricula at other levels. This book argues that unless issues such as the curriculum and the suitability of methods and materials used are tackled, and the basis for an objective-based curriculum questioned, then this high level assessment will, by default, become the focus of schools' attention.

There can be no better starting point in the enterprise of questioning and reformulation, than the work of Bruner and Stenhouse, who have outlined the importance of process rather than content in the curriculum. Until recently the opponents of process in the curriculum argued that basic skills were important and that children – particularly those with special needs – should not leave school without a survival level in these skills. However, such a view is increasingly less tenable in post-industrial society. Now, for the first time in over a century, the views of educationists such as Rousseau, Montessori and Froebel are no longer dissonant with the needs of society.

Curriculum for Special Needs in a Changing Society

It is the responsibility of all those who teach, particularly those in the area which has been labelled 'special needs', to make the work which they undertake in schools relevant. In order for this to occur, the ideas of those who put forward a process-centred curriculum have to be meshed with the ideas of those who appear to be far-sighted enough to sense the fundamental changes that are occurring in society. These changes are clearly due to the accelerating progress of technology. Toffler (1985) indicated that the survival of any organisation in the future will depend more and more on the ability of its members to communicate with one another, to think creatively and inventively, to be able to adapt to new situations and to find imaginative solutions to problems. This presents a challenge for our traditional system of education.

While many of these ideas have already been adopted by teachers, the dominating influence of an outdated curriculum is still evident to those who regularly visit schools. Plowden and Bullock were both guiding beacons in reforming the curriculum in primary education, yet as systematic studies of primary classes show, practices such as grouping – which occur in primary education and which are *ostensibly* geared towards fostering communication and cooperation etc. – mask far more traditional curricula and aims. In many classrooms, for example, children are seated in groups even when the tasks being undertaken are of an individual nature.

Given the new and widely expanding practices which are occurring in special needs, there is the opportunity for a fundamental re-evaluation of the kinds of skills which all children need, and of the context in which they may learn them. First, there must be the acceptance that the mainstream curriculum *is* the special curriculum. Integration cannot occur while some children are still engaged on a different topic from the main body of the class. Allied to this must be the notion that curriculum reform is inextricably linked with an analysis of the kinds of difficulties which children so often experience in our classrooms. Second, methods of assessing for special needs have to change fundamentally. At present they still identify and crystallise problems within children rather than problems within situations. Third, methods for organising the classroom have to change. Most classrooms are still organised for the single teacher in a segregated setting yet, as we have seen, the past few years have brought both larger numbers of children with special needs, as well as larger numbers of the personnel associated with those children into the mainstream classroom.

What are Special Needs Anyway?

Much of the discussion which has taken place about special needs and about the aims and goals of education generally, has centred around the concept of *basics* and *basic skills*. Indeed, this concept was at the centre of Callaghan's Great Debate on education in the late 1970s. Much of society's call on education rests in the concept of basic skills and it is necessary to question this concept in order for there to exist any meaningful understanding of the goals and aims of education generally.

Basic skills, as the term is generally understood, comprise the three Rs of reading, writing and arithmetic which form the grounding of society's requirements of an educated workforce. Assuming for a moment that these are indeed what society requires of its members in the late twentieth century, let us examine the way in which schools have organised themselves in order to produce members who are competent in the basic skills. These skills, as already outlined, have been the dominant feature of the curriculum of our schools over the last century. Yet schools have not been conspicuous in their ability to produce a workforce which is literate and numerate. Many would say that children leaving school at the age of sixteen are unable to cope with even the most basic levels of literacy and numeracy. Sir Keith Joseph has said that forty per cent of school leavers are barely competent in these skills. Given that children have spent ten years in compulsory schooling, one wonders why schools are so often turning out youngsters incapable in the basic skills areas. The inability of schools to produce children who are able to function in these supposedly important ways is thrown into sharp relief when we look at ways in which other systems of education are more successful and more efficient at producing these basic skills.

Take, for example, the work of Paulo Freire in Latin America who has shown that illiterate peasants are able to learn these basic skills in a matter of six weeks. The key component in their ability to learn was the fact that they were motivated. Perhaps what takes ten years without motivation can be accomplished in six weeks with motivation. A second example indicates just how far the organisation of our schooling and the professional structures which have built up to surround the profession of education in fact inhibit the effectiveness of education in fulfilling its goals adequately. This example is taken from the recent studies of parental involvement with children's reading, where it has been shown that if parents are involved with their children's reading, children can make phenomenal progress in a way that even large amounts of help at school would not be able to achieve.

What appears to be clear from both these examples is the fact that, given changes in the way that education is both conceived and organised, children and young people *are* capable of making extraordinary progress. Perhaps the fact that such progress is considered extraordinary is to do with the limited expectations which have grown up around schooling. It is not the fault of teachers that schooling is ineffective in these terms; society creates expectations and goals for education (as expressed, for example, in Callaghan's debate) which are set in a context which render those goals unattainable. By far the most important factor in deciding whether a child learns something is whether she/he learns it in a one-to-one setting (Bloom, 1984). Yet teachers are supposed to provide teaching in classes of more than thirty children. As far as one-to-one help is concerned, school is unlikely to provide such help successfully without structural reorganisation. And without reappraisal of the traditions which accompany schooling – such as the exclusion of parents – goals will forever be unattainable.

However, the basic skills of the late 1980s and onwards will not be those rote skills about which the Great Debate centred. If the analysis of Toffler is correct, these skills will be the kind of skills which have always been valued by liberal educators, but which have usually been rejected because they have been seen as dissonant with the needs of society. In fact, the new skills are not so much skills as abilities: creativity, the ability to work as part of a group, the ability to work independently, the ability to think imaginatively and the ability to communicate and to use language effectively.

If the new changes are bringing a reappraisal of the nature of basic skills, it is good news for that portion of the school population that has ever been labelled special. For it is they who have paid the penalty for being least suited to the traditional system. It is they who have been labelled 'thick', 'unintelligent', 'unmotivated', 'lazy', 'stroppy', or 'maladjusted' for failing to make sense of the curriculum or systems of organisation for which they could find no reference point in their everyday lives. This point can be illustrated by drawing on a vignette of education in a special school in Holland. First, it should be stated that the education system in Holland is highly segregated; nevertheless, within this segregation teachers are well resourced and are encouraged to embark on imaginative and innovative schemes of curriculum reform. In a school for children with behaviour difficulties, children go to 'video classes' where they are responsible for planning filming sessions, acting, filming, editing and so forth. The school takes particularly difficult children, yet as the teacher in charge of the classes remarks, 'We have no behaviour problems in this class.' It is immediately possible to see a number of reasons for the fact that behaviour problems are not experienced here: the curriculum is conspicuously relevant and is not broken down artificially into subject areas; learning is not expected to take place within the classroom walls (so restrictive of free discussion, flexible grouping and imagination) but rather takes place in small groups in the hall, the corridors, outside – indeed anywhere that appears to be appropriate at the time. The medium (i.e. video and filming) has relevance for the age that these children are living in and is thereby able to carry all the various messages that we would hope it to carry. Perhaps more important, though, is a point which is related to all these other points: the teacher in this instance had not responded to these children's needs by looking in intense detail at the children and asking himself, 'How can I diagnose these children's problems?' Rather, he had fundamentally restructured his teaching.

We have seen then that special needs do not necessarily reside *within* children (although clearly in a small minority of children there may be some disabling condition which may require special adaptations to the physical environment in the school or the classroom). For the vast majority of children about whom the Warnock Report was concerned – the twenty per cent of the school population – special needs exist because of the way in which education has developed over the last century, protected from children who did not fit by an elaborate system of special education.

Clearly, changes are necessary if schools are to meet society's future requirements. The possibilities for such changes exist but schools are often daunted by the difficulties involved in their development and subsequent implementation. Many fresh initiatives have petered out or fallen by the wayside because of lack of motivation, time and commitment. While it is true that lack of time and resources frequently produce a lowering of staff morale, it is important to realise that the chief contribution to the success of any new approach is made through the degree of staff commitment and the way in which it is sustained. The changes of attitude that the commitment might require are arguably the most important and most difficult to implement. The most necessary changes have to come from within the school and not be imposed upon it. At the same time, teachers at the heart of the education system, in the classroom and dealing on a daily basis with the concerns of children, are the people who, most of all, can perceive the hour by hour effects on pupils of under achievement and failure. The question of how to build upon achievement and divert the effects of failure into constructive learning channels is one that needs to be addressed by teachers themselves.

In order to do this effectively, a whole school approach needs to be adopted not only to organise curriculum development, but also to ensure that staff are fully aware of the need for changing curricula and methods, and understand fully the purposes behind such change. In-service education is an important element here. The authors of this book demonstrate clearly that many of the learning difficulties experienced by children do not necessarily reside within them, but can often be attributable to the situations in which they are placed and the demands that are made upon them within that situation. To consider some children as being 'below normal' in any subject poses the question, Who and what is normal? This immediately involves comparison, and in comparing one pupil with another it is usually the case to place the cause of the difficulty within the pupil. It is quite another matter to ask the question, Why are these pupils having difficulty with this subject? Such a question can give rise to answers that are concerned not only with what is going on inside the children but also with what is going on around them (Bines, 1986).

We need to consider involving children in activities which lead to constructive learning, and in this book we have attempted to look at the processes of learning and of meeting individual children's needs through key curricular areas where methods and resources are more appropriately utilised. The focus is on the curriculum and its development through a whole school approach. The nature of basic skill requirements has to be given greater consideration by schools as a whole and by individual teachers in providing suitable materials together with appropriate activities and methods to go with these materials. Thus, in looking at the areas which are the traditional domain of the special needs teacher, those areas are now placed within the context of the mainstream classroom and the mainstream curriculum. Placing skills within the mainstream brings in its wake the necessity for an appraisal of materials and their presentation to enable *all* children to develop a higher skill performance level. When considering, for example, how to help children become more independent in their work and more able to ask informed questions, an appraisal of teaching methods must follow. In such an appraisal, the organisation and management of both materials and methods must be given priority.

The approaches outlined in this book do not claim to be the only way of achieving a position where teachers can feel satisfied that they are beginning to reach out and succeed with children of all abilities. It is hoped, however, that it will provide an opportunity for teachers to consider forms of organisation and styles of teaching that will enable all children to meet the needs of the developing society more effectively.

The introduction of the Education Reform Act will impose changes on teachers and pupils. It is clear that it will force changes in teaching methods. A national curriculum, with tests at the ages of seven, eleven, fourteen and sixteen, is bound to create a more competitive climate in education, in which teaching becomes more formal. This is a matter of some concern for those of us who are trying to meet special needs wherever they occur. The Bill, as it is drafted at the time of writing, says very little about special needs. It is possible that with its emphasis on testing it may well resurrect the kind of atmosphere which those who work in special needs know is so damaging to children's confidence. It will create divisions – winners and losers.

This book has been concerned with access to the curriculum of all pupils, and thus encourages teachers to reflect upon the nature and diversity of learning needs, and the management and organisation of an environment through which many of those needs could more satisfactorily be met. Teachers, as professionals, need to be fully aware of the implications and outcomes of any change that is taking place. It is they who carry the responsibility to ensure that the desire to create 'good schools' does not fall into the trap of modelling such schools on the images of the past. It is to the twenty first century that educationists must address themselves and, in so doing, they have to become fully conversant with, and committed to, methods which will enable *all* children as individuals to achieve to their own highest standards.

References

BINES, H. (1986) *Redefining Remedial Education*. London: Croom Helm.
BLOOM, B.S. (1984) 'The search for methods of group instruction as effective as one to one tutoring', *Educational Leadership*, May, 4-17.
GEEN, A.G. (1985) 'Team teaching in the secondary schools of England and Wales', *Educational Review*, 37, 1, 29-38.
TOFFLER, A. (1985) *The Adaptive Corporation*. Aldershot: Gower.
TOURAINE, A. (1971) *The Post-industrial Society*. New York: Random House.

Index

Index